FOLLOW THE SUN

Other books by Arthur Marshall

Nineteen to the Dozen

Girls will be Girls

I Say!

I'll let you know
(Musings from 'Myrtlebank')

Smile Please
(Further Musings from 'Myrtlebank')

Life's Rich Pageant

Sunny Side Up

Edited by Arthur Marshall

New Statesman Competitions 1946–54

Salome, Dear, *not* in the Fridge

Never Rub Bottoms with a Porcupine

Whimpering in the Rhododendrons

Giggling in the Shrubbery

FOLLOW THE SUN

A further selection
of the writings of

Arthur Marshall

Edited by
Peter Kelland

Introduced by
Frank Muir

SINCLAIR-STEVENSON

First published in Great Britain by
Sinclair-Stevenson Limited
7/8 Kendrick Mews
London   SW7 3HG, England

Copyright previously published material © Arthur Marshall

Copyright this edition © 1990 Arthur Marshall's literary estate and Peter Kelland

Reprinted 1990

The editor, Peter Kelland, and the publishers, Sinclair-Stevenson, are very grateful
for the kind cooperation of the *Sunday Telegraph* and *New Statesman and Society*, in whose
pages a number of these pieces first appeared. The section entitled *Sunday Best*
consists of *Sunday Telegraph* pieces. In the section entitled *French for Beginners*, the short
passages from Nancy Mitford's *Voltaire in Love* and Richard Holmes' *Footsteps* are
reprinted by kind permission of Peters, Fraser and Dunlop and Hodder and
Stoughton publishers. *The Crooked Bat* and *Royal Mail* were included in books
published by Hamish Hamilton. We thank them and also any other newspapers or
periodicals which commissioned writing from Arthur Marshall reproduced here and
which we have been unable to identify.

A CIP Record for this title is available from the British Library
ISBN: 1 85619 022 6

Typeset by Colset Private Limited, Singapore
Printed and bound in Great Britain by
Clays Ltd, St Ives plc.

CONTENTS

Contents

Contents

LIST OF ILLUSTRATIONS

The photographs are between pages 118 and 119

Prep school days — dressed for the camera.
Cambridge days — dressed for the stage.
Stealing the show?
Oundle school staff. Arthur still holds centre stage.
At the time of his first radio broadcast.
On Active Service.
With Leslie Phillips and Terry Thomas, in the south of France.
At the controls of an Inter-City 125 train. (*Evening Standard, photograph by Graham Morris.*)
Call My Bluff, with Frank Muir and Robert Robinson. (*BBC.*)
All Star Secrets, with Michael Parkinson. (*London Weekend Television.*)
With Prunella Scales, raising funds for the Arts Theatre, Cambridge.
At a *Yorkshire Post* book signing. (*Yorkshire Post Newspapers Ltd, Leeds.*)
At 'Myrtlebank'.
In the garden.
On holiday in Florida with Peter Kelland.
Indian Summer — dressed for the camera. (*Photograph by Navana Studios, Exeter*).

The photograph on the back of the jacket is by courtesy of the BBC.

INTRODUCTION
by Frank Muir

Once, as I was sitting in Arthur Marshall's dressing-room relaxing before a recording of the television game *Call My Bluff*, Arthur suddenly said to me in his disarmingly charming voice: 'You know, I have always regarded you as a kind of university don *manqué*. Failed but undismayed.' This took a bit of digesting, and when he asked me how I regarded *him* I took a count of eight before replying. 'I think,' I said, 'that I have always thought of you as an unofficial English sunbeam.'

And I meant it as a compliment. My lasting memory of Arthur is of him in mid-chuckle, eyes aglow with that old stuff which we used to call merriment, and chins a-wobble. During most of his long life he had delighted above all else in making merry and being the cause of merriment in others.

On one of the late Russell Harty's television chat-shows, Russell made an effort to discover whether there was a serious intent behind Arthur's merry-making; a social message lurking beneath the flippancy. Arthur described the moment later in another of our pre-recording dressing-room sessions: 'I briskly threw away the frivolous mask,' he said to me, 'and, speaking in all sincerity and from the heart, said to Mr Harty: "I regard myself as being the Jeanette MacDonald of the prose world." '

This was a deeply Arthur-like remark: modest, funny and featuring one of those faintly bizarre luminaries of show-business in whom Arthur took great delight (he later began a book review in the *New Statesman* with a perfectly serious

1

debate on the question: 'In which of her many films did Jeanette MacDonald actually sing *loudest*?').

This was a mile away from satire. It was the gentle mocking of a star whose harmless films Arthur loved for their unlikelihood but whose promotion into a major world star, some way above the level of her competence, was viewed by Arthur with hilarity.

He was an aficionado of show-biz. The pre-war world of theatre and Hollywood, glittering and wittily bitchy, was his delight. He remained a lover of that world long after he became part of it, indeed until he died.

He became a performer because he developed a kind of humour which in those days was unique and much welcomed. In the early 1930s he was a teacher at Oundle school and he happened upon the schoolgirl stories of Angela Brazil which he found irresistibly funny when read aloud. From these readings he went on to write little three-minute sketches which he delivered in the guise of a stern gym or botany mistress. Between 1931 and 1934 he had written hundreds of these 'turns', as they were called, and he came to be much in demand at show-business parties. At one of these he met a producer from the BBC and he began his professional career as a female impersonator on the late-night radio revue 'Charlot's Hour', with such established stars as Frances Day, Douglas Byng and Ralph Lynn. Arthur was the world's first wireless drag act.

The charming and funny young Arthur was invited everywhere. He spent long weekends at Somerset Maugham's villa in the South of France, he spent months with the Lunts in New York. Everybody in the theatre knew Arthur.

But he was no social cuckoo. Came the war and he became an Intelligence officer, eventually Lieutenant-Colonel Marshall, MBE, on General Eisenhower's Staff.

The breakthrough into prose came as early as 1935. Raymond Mortimer, then literary editor of the *New Statesman*, asked Arthur to review a clutch of schoolgirl stories for the Christmas edition of the magazine. The review was a huge success and Arthur's annual round-up of schoolgirls' books became one of the magazine's most popular Christmas features. This led to Arthur writing a column for the *New Statesman* and, when that was ended, for the *Sunday Telegraph*. Then came collections of his pieces published in book form, a volume of autobiography, appearances on television on *Call My Bluff* . . .

The irony is that in the world of broadcast humour in the late 1980s it was Arthur who was the Alternative Comedian. The late '80s will probably go down in the books as the era of young writers and comics appealing to young viewers and readers with a stunning display of aggressive, sexual and politically simplistic comedy nurtured on the students' union circuit. But, for those for whom this sort of comedy ceased to appeal much after the first excitement, Arthur's charming, intelligent, well-read, witty, *affectionate* humour came as a breath of fresh air.

Arthur's comedy was not political nor a vehicle for social comment. And had I suggested to him that his writings might benefit from a whiff of sex he would have rolled up his eyes, murmured 'Oh, Buster — *Tiens!*' and that would have been that. Arthur knew what he was doing and he did it in exemplary fashion. He wrote the way he talked and he talked the way he lived and, in its own quiet way, it all worked beautifully.

In retrospect, dear Uncle Arthur was perhaps the last flowering of what Addison and Steele called Polite Comedy, which they pioneered nearly three hundred years ago. Instead of the character assassinations of the political humour of the day, and the even more vicious personal attacks licensed by the classical theory that comedy should remedy personal faults through mockery, Addison and Steele laid down that humour should be happy and should laugh at the odd idiosyncracies, accurately observed, of good people.

Which is exactly what Arthur did all his writing life. Furthermore his humorous style was original, his view of the world about him was distinct and unique.

And those qualities are here before us. To be enjoyed.

FRANK MUIR
Surrey, 1990

FOREWORD
by Peter Kelland

When Arthur Marshall published his delightful auto-biography, *Life's Rich Pageant*, in 1984 there were very many people, myself included, who felt that the book could be faulted. It was too short.

For example, the final chapter, 'Indian Summer', took his story to 1970 and covered, or did not cover, if you prefer, the next twelve years in a mere six pages. It was during this time, of course, and thanks mainly to the power of television, that Arthur became a national figure, recognised in the street, in trains and taxis, in Sainsbury's and in the Bank and forever greeted with a nudge and a 'Look isn't that. . . you know . . . the one on telly . . .?' Asked whether he objected to publicity, Arthur replied: 'Oh, no. You see they always come up with a smile.'

Television's *Call My Bluff* was the chief instigator of all this interest and the most persistent question that he was asked was: 'Do you find that appearing on *Call My Bluff* increases your vocabulary?' Of course the words used are so strange that they would never crop up in ordinary conversation and Arthur's answer was always the same, so much so that we had to be very careful not to catch each other's eyes as he replied: 'Well no, not really. You see, quite recently we had "krankle".' (I think he made this up.) 'Well, krankle is the name for a special type of nail in a steeplejack's boot. Now, the chances of actually meeting a steeplejack walking down the street are far from rosy. Would you know one if you saw one? And, if you did, and were to say to him: "Excuse me, but how

5

are your krankles?'' you would be thought to be very odd, at the least!'

I believe there are two reasons why Arthur glossed over so quickly the more recent events in his life. In the first place, before the very successful publication of his *Life's Rich Pageant*, he was unsure whether anyone would wish to read about his own rather ordinary life. He found the idea mildly preposterous, but conceded that, just perhaps, a brief account of various incidents in the 1920s and 1930s might be of interest to some of the older generation. The 1970s and 1980s, however, were by their very nature too clear, or so he thought, in the minds of others to warrant re-telling. And, secondly, I have a suspicion that Arthur's own memory, so brilliant when recalling rare episodes in his youth, had difficulty in pinning down with any accuracy what had happened the day before yesterday.

Nevertheless, happily seeming to have recovered from a minor heart attack, Arthur began, in the early summer of 1988, work on a second autobiography. Alas, he had barely started when his second and, in the end, overwhelming illness prevented him from making any further progress. The first two chapters, however, were more or less complete and, as in *Life's Rich Pageant*, begin with his father and move on to reminiscences of life with his grandparents in Essex and Devon, his Hampshire prep school and his first visit to France. The old memory was very much still there, and the chapters in question form the first section of this book.

I make no excuse for ending this collection with two favourite pieces from previous publications. As a fellow schoolmaster and keen cricketer (in reality Arthur loved the game too and no one became more incensed than he whenever England dropped a vital catch), I cannot resist *The Crooked Bat* (*Girls will be Girls*, 1974). A second favourite of ours was *Royal Mail* (*I Say!* 1977). The latter was subsequently translated into Russian as a totally serious indictment of royal behaviour! Such bizarre vignettes of life were always dear to

Foreword

Arthur's heart and I can still hear his chuckle as he counted his fee — in roubles.

For the rest we return to 'Indian Summer', that all too brief period when he thought he had retired and found instead that he was in constant demand from all branches of the media. Here you will find a wide variety of articles written for a wide variety of newspapers and magazines — some of them more than ten years old — and all, I hope, reminding us, alas for the last time, of that laughter and irrepressible sense of humour which overflowed into Arthur's writing and into every second of every day that he lived.

PETER KELLAND
Devon, 1990

LET ME BE YOUR FATHER!

LET ME BE YOUR FATHER! Thus ran, in my youth, an urgent plea, in a *Strand Magazine* advertisement, to join a comprehensive correspondence course in business studies. To back up the somewhat impertinent suggestion there was a photograph of a middle-aged man vaguely looking like Mr Baldwin (and dead presumably) pointing a finger and beaming encouragement. In return for what was then quite a tidy sum of money he undertook to off-load explanatory literature that would take the applicant in a trice straight to the top of the business tree, admired by all in the office and chatting with the boss on level terms. Foreign students were said to be enchanted by Dad and to join up in droves.

Rum in many ways though my own father was, I had no wish at all to change him. In all matters of importance he was entirely reliable, and, if he found it difficult to display much parental affection, well that was just the way he was. And to my mother and me he was an endless source of mild amusement and innocent merriment.

For example, one week-end afternoon he had had occasion to call on a senior Wheel Works employee at his home in Pimlico. He arrived back for our Sunday tea in Barnes much put out, for the man, as my father was about to leave, meaning well no doubt, had said: 'Do you want to visit the Gents?' 'What a vulgar thing to ask! I mean to say! Well really!' spluttered my father. And anyway, he went on, 'Gents' implied a row of upright porcelain urinal stalls periodically flushed from a tank and smelling of disinfectant, if you were

9

lucky, and altogether a most improbable amenity in a small Pimlico house.

My mother, sensing the possibility of some fun, asked what the employee should have said, and then herself suggested: 'Do you want to retire?', although to some people that might be taken wrongly to imply professional retirement from work, personal details of which in this case the man had no right to ask. She then, careful to appear innocent, added that she had once heard a lavatory referred to as 'the what's-it'. 'Do you require the what's-it?' Would that have done? Fortunately the nauseating 'littlest room' had not yet arrived from America, nor the extremely misleading 'bathroom'.

In the end my father decided that in similar circumstances the best way out would be to say: 'Would you. . . . er . . .?' accompanying this masterpiece with a sort of vague gesture in the general direction of Relief. My mother, remembering that our house boasted three lavatories, at once merrily sketched at a wild windmill of encouraging gestures in all directions, but then, seeing that my father was getting huffy, cheered him (I must add 'probably', for this I don't actually remember) with the last of the Gentleman's Relish sandwiches. He was a happy muncher and could usually be calmed with food. And it had been a jolly ten minutes.

My father had a sense of humour, but it was robust rather than subtle. In the childhood days of which I write, we spent much of our time sticking our tongues out, usually in mocking derision of somebody or something, but sometimes at the request of the family doctor, who also required us to say 'ninety-nine' quite a lot. My father, who disliked being told to do anything, was, too, once asked to say 'ninety-nine' and, finding himself to be in waggish mood, replied with a loud 'one hundred and twenty-eight' confidently expecting chuckles. But our medical man, Dr Otway of Barnes, being on his rounds and pushed for time, was far from amused. 'What a dry old stick Otway is,' remarked my father after the doctor had left.

One of our three lavatories was of course a servant's one lurking in gloomy surroundings next to the copper, a then indispensable domestic device for boiling all clothes and linen that required boiling. Although both WC and toilet were freely available, things were far from affluent and my father discouraged extravagances by a prudent mania for saving money. Nevertheless we had two maids and a cook and an odd-job man for Sundays and this was, in those days, an entirely normal middle-class complement, while away in Ilfracombe my maternal grandmother's maids seemed an endless line as they fell in for Morning and Evening Prayers. There was also a gardener and an indoor male servant called Burnham, not grand enough to be called a butler, but doing a butler's job. Or doing this as far as his dreadful tipsiness and clumsiness and illness allowed. He was, as all but one could see, a rogue, but, in my grandmother's eyes, he was perfection, and was referred to at all times as 'my poor old Burnham'. He wheezed quite a lot and, not surprisingly, had gout.

The house was not far from the coast, the dangerously rocky North Devon shore of the proximity of which mariners on dark and foggy nights were warned by blasts from an ear-splitting foghorn, which was the signal for my grandmother to say: 'Poor old Burnham's chest is bad tonight.' Constant attempts to pinpoint for her the actual cause of the din fell on the deafest of ears, and one foggy evening my poor cousin Madge was even bidden to go and rub, unlovely task, Burnham's chest.

My cousin Madge, twenty or so years older than I, was resilient at all times and I loved her dearly. Relatively speaking, my grandparents were her Aunt Kate and Uncle Arthur and she and my mother shared a Derbyshire grandmother, which made us all cousins of one sort or another. My grandparents were old and frail and Madge, in the kindness of her heart, acted as a secretary-companion to them, her geniality proving equal to the various strains put upon her. In her youth Madge had been a notable tomboy, and on a trip we made across the Bristol Channel to her Welsh home town she delighted in showing me the various spots in Tenby where she, in her own words, had come a purler off her bike. The tomboy had become in due course what used to be called a 'handsome woman'. And handsome she seemed to me, manly even, with blue eyes and a charming smile. Her reddish hair was very striking, sometimes cut fairly short and sometimes grown so long that she could, if she wished (and this seems to have been a popular Victorian pastime) have sat on it. After the last war she came to live near my mother in our Devon village, where she was loved and respected by all.

Ilfracombe Sundays were bleak in the extreme. No Sunday papers were ever permitted and even one's ordinary reading had to be of a devotional nature. My grandfather was in holy orders and the routine on the Sabbath was punishing indeed. The Communion Service was at eight and Family Prayers at nine, with all the servants present except, for obvious reasons, cook whose spiritual well-being was sacrificed in favour of fried sausages. There was Matins at eleven and lunch at one to which numerous pink-cheeked curates were invited, with the chat, such as it was, confined to church affairs. Sunday School was at three, evensong at six and Family Prayers at bed-time. God, though sometimes a little unreasonable in his demands, must really have been quite pleased with us.

The evening devotion at six sometimes contained a merry treat for, occasionally, dear Madge, who was 'musical', was pressed into service when the regular organist was absent for some reason or another. Madge always had the greatest difficulty in counting the number of hymn verses she had played. She frequently thundered out, and with joyous abandon and every stop in use, an extra verse for which there were no words. My grandfather, looking pained, sang the last

12

verse over again and threw in a hurried 'amen' in case dear old
Madge should be inspired to play vigorously on.

Madge, a card if ever there was one, was also made
responsible for arranging the altar flowers. These were
brought to the house by the florist on Saturday morning and
were solemnly blessed by my grandfather in his study, with the
intention that they then, in their aura of holiness, go straight to
the church. But Madge briskly stuffed them into her bicycle
basket and smartly joined us in the town for coffee, the flowers
being shoved under the table, where they got hacked about a
bit. When my grandmother, as frequently happened, said that
she thought that the altar flowers 'looked a little droopy'
(gladioli), one had to be careful not to catch Madge's eye.

Without going to the same extremes, my paternal grandmother, living in Essex, also considered it sinful to read a
Sunday newspaper, and resisted doing so up to her death in
1933. Her knowledge of the newspaper world was slim, and
she supposed that loyal reporters were up all night and scribbl-
ing into the Sabbath (perhaps they indeed do). And if not
reporters, what about newspaper train drivers, newsagents
and those who deliver, all of them busily at it on a day that
should be totally holy and work-free? No good Christian
should encourage such practices.

However, my grandmother was kind and, not wishing to
thrust her beliefs on others, dutifully ordered the more
reputable Sunday papers for friends staying in the house, for
the servants and, of course, for us, her relations. We pounced
on them with joy for they often contained sensational
matters — a murder, perhaps, or a daring jewel robbery, or a
romantic elopement, then quite 'the thing', of a couple in high
society (*Peeress dodges reporters at Dover*).

My grandmother, whom I greatly loved, and despite her
faith, was but human and seeing me goggling excitedly away
at some compelling item, used to be able to shelve quite easily,
and for the time being, her high principles. Looking extremely
guilty, she would sidle up to me and say: 'What's that you're

reading, dear?', swiftly adding: 'Any further news of that awful murder in Fulham?' 'Oh, yes,' one happily said. 'They've found the head, wrapped in a tea-towel and dumped in a neighbour's dust-bin!' 'Oh, how dreadful! Now run along, darling, and get ready for church.'

If many of these goings-on seem quaint now, they seemed perfectly normal to me at the time and in no way did they prepare me for the shocks that awaited me in my first boarding school. Pre-war prep schools were famous for their oddities, in which connection the one I attended, Stirling Court on the Hampshire coast, could be called run-of-the-mill. Like many other schools of the period, it prospered or failed according to the drawing power of the headmaster and Stirling Court, still prospering but in a new location, has been extremely lucky. Few prep schools had any sort of waiting list (the better public schools, with lists a mile long, could face the future with confidence) and the poorer ones amongst them could collapse almost overnight. Indeed some, alas, still do, and on my way to and from London by car in the 1960s I watched with sadness the fairly rapid disintegration of one such school in Wiltshire. Two games of rugger giving way to one (and only twelve a side at that), few masters on view, grass becoming too long, goal-posts sagging and the field eventually abandoned to developers; finally the school buildings themselves put up for sale and, unoccupied, stripped by vandals. A sorry sight, and all in a couple of years or so.

One of the many mysteries connected with Stirling Court was why the food, in addition to being inadequate in quantity and usually unappetising to gaze upon, should also be so tasteless. My friend Williamson, an intrepid investigator, penetrated the kitchen regions at a time when the culinary staff (one obese cook) was absent and reported that nowhere could he find any salt. We knew all about salt. It constantly popped up both in church and in Scripture classes. If the salt has lost his savour, wherewith shall it be salted? A real poser of a question. And why 'his' one wondered? And could salt really just lose its potency? Puzzling. Williamson, on a week-end visit to his Portsmouth home, secured a packet of salt and subsequently left it, as both a rebuke and a suggestion, on the kitchen table, but, even if the cook made use of it, it didn't seem to do much for the watery cabbage and *al dente* carrots. Our 'amens' following 'For what we are about to receive . . .' lacked a certain enthusiasm.

Another enigma concerned the human form and, in particular, nakedness. Hot baths, supervised by Matron, were weekly and Friday-nightly and entirely communal. Naked and unashamed and for ever flicking each other with towels ('Oh, do shut up, Letchworth minor'), there were no anatomical secrets possible, or needed to be.

However, it was quite another matter when dressing in the morning ('Has anyone seen my back collar stud?') or undressing for bed. On these occasions intimate regions had to be, at all costs, kept fully draped and hidden (removing one's underpants provided many a perilous moment). At the slightest hint of a wobbling pink area, or an appendage not normally on view, the done thing was to shriek '*Sights*' and add the culprit's name (surname only of course), and all in a manner which, even at the time, I thought to be awful and of which, in retrospect, I am deeply ashamed. But one shouted with the rest.

Come to think of it, all the bother could so easily have been avoided. How sad it is to think of Adam and Eve in the Garden of Eden fiasco, in which nakedness played its part. If only Eve had said that apples set her teeth on edge and that, as regards her vitamin C intake, she would much prefer a few of those luscious-looking purple things from that tree over there — the fruit with the very large and seemingly useless leaves.

Do young people at boarding schools still suffer from what was called 'pink eye'? How popular is, to give it its official name, conjunctivitis? And when I say popular, I mean 'well liked' for it brought great advantages with it. 'As pants the hart for cooling streams' we sang in chapel but, at the merest

15

rumour of an outbreak of the disease, what we were all really panting for was pink eye.

In those days it meant instant withdrawal from work and games and a delightfully restful period in the sick-room, with Matron at her friendly best ('I've managed to scrounge you a couple of custard creams') and what hotels refer to as 'full room service', for which a fairly trifling ocular inflammation and irritation was a small price to pay. Our hospital condition was indeed, as the medical bulletins have it, 'comfortable'.

An added enjoyment was, once safely installed, to hear distant sounds of scholastic activity, with its constant ups and downs and anxious moments ('Tell Devenish he's wanted in top study'). Meanwhile one sluiced away with an eye-bath and a solution of boric acid, or plain water if Matron wasn't hovering (a pity to clear the thing up too quickly). And if the disease got going in a really big way, school matches had to be cancelled, a deprivation that disappointed some of us more than others, mysteriously unselected as one was for the Fourth XV v Dumbleton (away). Which reminds me of the delicious smile which appeared on the late John Betjeman's face when, due to arrive back at his old prep school as Poet Laureate and in a helicopter, he realised that this machine was to land on the 'square' and that cricket would, perforce, have to be abandoned for the day.

Sadly out of touch as I am nowadays with modern schools, I therefore know nothing of the current chilblain situation. I find it impossible to believe that winter chilblains, too, like so many other old-fashioned weaknesses, have virtually disappeared. From late October onwards their itching provided a daily and nightly (even worse) torture. My mother, seldom given to complain, but moved to action by my weekly epistolatory wails, once raised the subject with the authorities at Stirling Court and received by way of reply a letter of mild reproof stating that my chilblains were entirely due to the fact that I was not drying myself properly.

My mother was far too polite to answer 'Bunkum!' but

bunkum it certainly was, a judgement backed by the invaluable and widely admired medical section of *Pears Cyclopaedia* which clearly states that chilblains occur most often in young people who have 'insufficient nourishing food', three words which describe all too accurately the Stirling Court menus. The moment one arrived home for the hols and ate sustaining food, the chilblains instantly disappeared. QED, as one used triumphantly to write at the conclusion of some closely reasoned geometrical argument, the saucier boys saying that the letters stood for Quite Easily Done.

And there was another happy mathematical moment (few and far between I may say) when, at the end of some rubbish which involved x and y, one was encouraged to write a dismissive 'which is absurd'. We made free use of the phrase, our school life being full of wild absurdities ranging from the headmaster's wife's Sunday hats to most of the Old Testament.

And indeed to one of the prime treats of every summer term, which was to have a peep at Captain Hodgson's appendix scar. Appendicitis had come upon him suddenly and at lunchtime in the Easter term of 1921 when, faced with his portion of Irish stew (Tuesdays), he had given a sudden cry of anguish and had collapsed, Matron doing the necessary and much relishing the challenge. Removed from our midst, he was seen no more that term. I may say that cries of anguish at mealtimes were by no means a novelty though they did not always indicate appendicitis.

Captain Hodgson taught Geography and his temporary absence was covered by a local resident, Miss Fanshawe, whose claims to geographical knowledge appeared to be based on two week-end trips with her sister to Boulogne, her reminiscences of hectic Continental life being pretty tame when compared with the gallant and recently demobilised Captain's tales of Gallipoli and Flanders.

However, the start of the summer term saw him back again, fresh as paint and minus his appendix, an apparently quite useless piece of bodily equipment. (Perhaps the Creation had been a harder job than one thought?) We bathed daily in the icy Solent, a stretch of water coveniently provided with two tides and when it was the Captain's turn to take the expedition to the beach and after we had all sufficiently swum and dived and splashed each other ('Oh, do shut up, Lightbody!') it was Appendix Time and we all gathered eagerly round.

The scar display was conducted in the very seemliest of manners, the surrounding fleshy areas (rather hirsute one gathered) being tastefully concealed by two large orange-coloured bathing towels. And there, in the middle, was a conglomeration of clumsy-looking stitching and red and puckered skin, quite fascinating to behold, though a rather feeble boy called Meld said he felt faint. Williamson, whose father was a doctor, took a more professional view of the matter: 'Oh, yes. Quite a normal appendectomy. Nothing to get too excited about.'

FRENCH FOR
BEGINNERS

It was only very gradually in life that I became aware that there existed something called France. A place, apparently, to the knowledge of which I came by a roundabout route.

In 1914 my father, an engineer, was manager of The Pimlico Wheel Works, the firm's locality and purpose speaking for itself. Although King George V, by reputation not exactly one for setting the table in a roar, once jovially remarked that he lived in Pimlico, Buckingham Palace lying indeed within its boundaries, Pimlico did not in those days rank very highly as a provider of what property dealers call 'desirable residences' and so we lived in Barnes, a more socially acceptable district at no great distance and conveniently reachable by omnibus.

In my childhood a prime Sunday treat was, after Matins, to be taken in our rather dashing and bright yellow Metallurgique car to the Works, get filled up with ginger-beer and pat-a-cake biscuits by the kind employee on duty (the place was manned day and night) and then be pushed up and down in one of the goods wagons in which, I suppose, my father's wheels when constructed were profitably moved by rail to where they would do most good.

In mid-July 1914, when I was four years old, my father went on business to Belgium. Presumably the Walloons were in need of better, perhaps even *rounder*, wheels and such as only Pimlico could provide. He returned a few days before 4 August and I well remember adult conversation in the home containing phrases such as 'a narrow squeak' and 'cutting it fine' and 'a near thing'. But what was this 'Belgium'? At the age of four one was a constant question-putter but the only answer given me about my father's trip and his foreign whereabouts was that 'Belgium' was next to 'France', whatever that might be. And later on I heard that Belgium had been tremendously 'plucky', seemingly a word in its favour.

From that dread August on, war fever was in the air, everywhere were to be seen maps of the Continent, covered in dotted lines and arrows and tiny flags indicating Us, and little by little one gathered that France was quite a large section of land more or less opposite England, with water in between. I was an eager reader of *Punch*, and its cartoons, often by Bernard Partridge, revealed that La France was female, as also, by gender and in French, were Britain and, *how* unsuitably, Germany, and France was personified by a sturdy and be-clogged peasant woman wearing a Napoleonic hat and waving either a scythe or a flag and with an expression on her face that seemed to indicate that her income tax demand had just arrived and that she intended to query it. Defiant and cross, in fact.

At the Froebel Institute, that paradise of pleasurable learning in Hammersmith, the kindergarten scholastic curriculum did not include the French language but when I moved on, aged seven, to Miss Wright's Ranelagh House School overlooking Barnes Common, French was all the rage, France by then having proved itself to be every bit as plucky, if not even more so, as stout-hearted Belgium. Our language teacher, Madame Croxford, whose 'Madame' was a courtesy title in the way that in those days a spinster cook improved her standing by calling herself Mrs Goodbody, believed in teaching by the Direct Method — not a word of English uttered in the classroom and the air thick with *Fermez la porte* and *Ouvrez vos livres* and, of course, *Taisez-vous*!

I took to it instantly, especially as Madame Croxford was very theatrically-minded and we did a lot of acting in French, such a good and enjoyable way for children to learn a language. On one occasion I was a heavily bearded French doctor examining a woman patient, my great friend Mary White obligingly feigning illness with a whitened face. I had strict instructions from Miss Wright not to apply the stethoscope indelicately to Mary's non-existent bosom but to her stomach, which I did with much eye-rolling and assorted cries of *Mon Dieu*! and *Oh, là là*!, followed by Gallic shrugs and noisy whistles (*sifflements*) of disbelief and dismay, before summoning an ambulance to take Mary instantly to hospital. The little scene had quite a success and we later performed it, not very tactfully perhaps, to a wardful of wounded soldiers.

Though we were quite well equipped orally in French, our written work was less impressive and it was on this, with future exam papers in mind, that they rightly concentrated at Stirling Court, the secrets of the language being revealed to us in a book, which I still have, by a Frenchman, a Monsieur Chardenal. In a preface which instantly showed that the writer was not English, we were advised to 'take every morning two or three verbs and as many sentences, and turn them mentally in every possible way, or at night in bed before sleeping', a sure way of inducing headaches during the day and insomnia at night. And it was at this point in my life that I began to wonder a little whether the French were, so to speak, *all right*.

It was the sentences for translation that did it. It was 1920, the war was over and 'they', with considerable help from others, had won, but in the sentences there was a boastfulness that was rather displeasing. I didn't mind things like 'My aunt's house is very much bigger than yours' for that might apply to anybody, but much was made both of the Eiffel Tower ('The tower's height exceeds that of all other foreign buildings') with not a word about its hideousness, and of Napoleon ('All Europe trembled before his victorious armies') with no mention at all of Wellington and humiliating defeat. And aware as one by then was of phrases such as 'cock-a-hoop' and 'cock of the walk' and 'to be a bit cocky', it seemed all too suitable that, to match Britain's bulldog and America's eagle, the French should have settled for *un coq* as their national emblem.

And there was something else. A Stirling Court contemporary called Brand had a naval father and spent his holidays in married quarters at the Portsmouth barracks. Mooning about one day in a petty officers' mess, where he obviously had no business to be, he had come upon a French magazine full of pictures of ladies who had forgotten to put their clothes on. There were also, he said, stories and anecdotes and illustrated advertisements for contraptions whose rubbery purpose remained a mystery. The magazine's name was *La Vie Parisienne* and clearly the publication came under the heading of Smut, against which we were warned at least twice a day. Though secretly much excited, some of us even urging Brand to pinch the thing when next he was there and let us all have a thrilling peep, one adopted outwardly a priggish attitude and notched up another minus mark on our neighbours' moral score-sheet.

My youthful doubts about their purity were increased by a curious chance. The French teaching at Stirling Court was of a high standard and, partly thanks to a text book assembled by the then Head of Modern Languages at Cheltenham College, we could manage quite complicated Cheltonian teasers such as 'Never go out on an empty stomach' (*Ne sortez jamais à jeun*) and another, which some of us thought not unfunny, 'I am anxious to show you my greenhouses' (*Je tiens à vous montrer mes serres*). Passing on to Oundle School, I quite soon won a French prize which turned out to be a handsomely bound copy of *A Wanderer in Paris* by E.V. Lucas, an author famous for wandering all over the shop and then writing profitably about it.

From early on a keen reader, I wasted no time in opening the book and wandering too. We begin with Mr Lucas's departure from England and arrival by train in Paris and at the Gare du Nord. And bless me, within an hour he has seen, 'written up in chalk on a public wall', a graffito which read

'*Vivent les femmes*!' The author chooses to regard the words as being 'in large emotional letters', possibly chalked up by 'a Parisian who desires the continuance of his joy as a lover'. I see no grounds at all for such a romantic interpretation and anyway, if the man was a true and genuine lover why did he not chalk up 'Vive Hortense!' or 'Vive Genevieve!' And all this at page two, with 262 more pages to go. This, however, was the last of the graffiti, as I was slightly sorry to find. A final thought. How, pray, can you identify 'a large emotional letter' when it's at home, or on a wall?

My father held gloomy views about French hygiene and cleanliness and had had an Experience on which his opinions were based. On that famous trip to Belgium, when he had escaped from old Jerry by the skin of his teeth, the weather was unusually hot and he had gone for a refreshing dip in a Brussels swimming-bath. The bath's owners, fastidious people obviously, had put up a notice requiring anybody of French nationality to sluice themselves down (it was long before the widespread use of showers) with several buckets of water before entering the bath. There was no such requirement for other nationalities, whose fragrance was, and rather rashly in some cases, assumed.

On this rather slim piece of evidence my father had erected a whole scaffolding of doubts and apprehensions, and I was therefore considerably surprised when in 1926 a French holiday was decided on and we proceeded to St Malo by boat and then took a car along the Brittany coast to our destination, St Lunaire.

To help us to alight from the Cross-Channel packet and to seize and manhandle our luggage and to rob us as far as was legally possible, an attacking force of blue-tunic-ed porters boarded the boat at St Malo. When writing about French males who earn their living by physical means, it used to be necessary to make use of the adjective 'swarthy', and swarthy our porter indeed was, though whether from birth or exposure to sun or just good old dirt, who could say? He whizzed us and our trunks through Customs and maintained a cheerful appearance and polite bearing until the time when my father presented him with what seemed to us to be an adequate, some might even say generous, tip. From the furious flow of invective that followed I could distinguish just the one word '*sale*', often used by Madame Croxford when requesting the owner of grubby hands to go and wash them. Otherwise the porter's effortless stream of words was incomprehensible and might even have floored Madame Croxford herself, and just as well I dare say. My mother, ever practical, said: 'Why don't we just continue to hand over francs until he stops screaming?', which is what we did.

We had made a night crossing and by the time we had settled in the car and had started off it was midday, the sacred hour when all French motorists stop and eat at the roadside huge quantities of bread and pâté. They also do other things that their presence in the car had not permitted and for these activities they face, for preference, the road. Well, why bother about concealment? We're all made the same way, aren't we? Well then! They certainly were on this occasion and, as we bowled past, facing the road. My father observed these watery achievements with a discouraged eye and his 'I told you so' look.

Arrival at our St Lunaire hotel did little to alter his estimation of our hosts for at once we became aware of that very distinctive mark of many French hotels. Smell. It wasn't entirely what one might call a smelly smell but one's thoughts did wander for a moment to drains. It is difficult to describe smells and impossible to describe tastes (a banana tastes like a banana). This was a weird mixture of carbolic soap and wet linen and imperfectly trained cats and long forgotten meals and old clothes and unopened windows. It was a fusty musty smell and I don't doubt that, on encountering it for the first time, and as the schoolboy that I then was, I supplied the dismissive word 'Pooh!' and a disgusted facial expression to go with it.

My father was at home accustomed to taking a hot bath every morning and at a fairly early hour and he was far from pleased to discover that the floor on which our bedrooms and about a dozen others lay had just the one bathroom. And it was locked. Anxious enquiries at the desk brought the information that, to obtain a bath, a bedroom bell must be pushed to summon the maid to unlock the bathroom to light the geyser to fill the bath to put out a towel, etc etc. And it was only after he had immersed himself on the first morning that my father discovered another hazard of most Continental hotels — no soap! Another bad mark.

My parents' command of the French language was limited to '*Oui*' and '*Non*' and numbers up to and including '*Dix*', though my mother had somewhere learnt '*Vraiment?*' with a rising inflection, a word of which she made frequent use at the end of long and incomprehensible harangues directed at her by a native and which made her appear to be an accomplished speaker. I was, therefore, with my Croxford background, pressed into service as interpreter and, on that first morning, an acquirer of soap. Approaching the rather formidable Madame behind the desk, I was tempted to show off by making use of a faultless Stirling Court subjunctive — *Il faut que mon père ait du savon* — but in the end I settled for something simpler. No good. Soap, I was informed, must be bought in a shop and so out we trailed to the *pharmacie* and tried to find a not too highly scented soap, my father strongly disapproving of scent ('foreign filth'). I hope that I have not given the impression that during all this activity my father was still in the bath. He had reluctantly removed himself — unsoaped, unwashed, unclean, as he considered himself to be, though in point of fact he was always fresh as a daisy and you could have safely eaten your lunch off him.

On our return to England we discovered that our close friends, a family called Bentley, had arranged what is called An Exchange, a system by which their son, Philip, went for a month to the *famille* Bourdon in Tours, a town popularly supposed to supply the 'best' French accent, whatever that might turn out to be, and in due course the Bourdon boy came to the Bentleys and their Berkshire accent for the same length of time. The French boy's Christian name was Richard and everybody learnt to pronounce it *Ree-shar*, feeling rather dashing and continental. He wore a knickerbocker suit throughout his stay and his knees were never exposed to public view for he refused to bathe (we used to splash happily about in a deepish section of the River Kennet) and, in addition to the suit, he wore a doleful expression for most of the time. He was a Catholic and on Sundays he had to be transported by a reluctant driver to the nearest Catholic church. His finger nails gleamed and glistened like anything and we were fairly sure that he polished them. Mr Bentley, even more insular than my father, referred to him as 'our encumbrance' and regretted the whole undertaking.

And so, what with one thing and another, I had good reason to feel apprehensive when, in 1928 and before going up to Cambridge, it was decided to send me to a French family in Grenoble where I could take the Summer Course for English Students at the University, become reasonably fluent and arrive at Cambridge with something of a head start. So to Grenoble I went, trembling slightly in my shoes.

But then, on my arrival in Savoy, all was suddenly changed . . . In the house in which I found myself all was cleanliness; even the kitchen, into which we sometimes peeped, was extremely spick and span. The establishment was run by the three Rolland sisters and a staff of two — cook and maid-of-all-work — and they provided beds, food, conversation and kindly advice for five or six foreign students at a time, and it was under this hospitable roof that I first came to know what really good French home cooking could be like. For example, there were, they told us, over a hundred different ways of serving potatoes. At home in England we had them boiled, baked, mashed and roasted. But the Rolland sisters prided themselves on ringing the changes. We had them sautéd with onion and, blended with cooked cabbage and any left-over bits of vegetable, we had them fried (our own good old bubble-and-squeak). We had them very thinly sliced and cooked in milk, we had them done with leeks, we had them Duchesse (attractively oven-browned). We had them blended with fragments of crisp and crinkled fried bacon. For baked potatoes there were many different fillings — cheese, egg, ham, mushroom — and our friendly hostesses smiled indulgently at us while we, in imitation of the witches' sailor's wife in *Macbeth*, munched and munched and munched, though in her case it was merely chestnuts (and we had them, too, as a poultry stuffing).

It took me no time at all to get used to the delightful French way of serving lettuce. At home and in childhood I had been warned by my parents, both of them keen trencher-folk, that certain foods — and they mentioned in particular oysters, olives, caviare and foie gras — were an 'acquired taste' and I could not expect to enjoy them right away. I found the warning to be, in my case, faulty. No edible in my life has been more delicious than the first oyster (in Rules, Maiden Lane) or my first spoonful, toast-seated, of caviare (in Monte Carlo). And so it was with French salad dressing, that delicious mixture of olive oil and lemon juice and what used to be called 'condiments', all with a good dash of sugar. This the Rolland sisters provided almost daily to go with large bowls of lettuce, served as a separate course as is often the way with French vegetables, and quite right so to honour them. After all, in Yorkshire that superb pudding is similarly treated before the roast beef makes its appearance.

Tastes in food vary, with the French as with any other race, and in *Voltaire in Love* Nancy Mitford has provided a culinary passage that is not for the squeamish or the soft-hearted. Voltaire, desperately ill and on a journey with his secretary, Longchamp, has eaten virtually nothing for a week and is contemplating death. What food might just possibly tempt him back to life?

When at last he was comfortably in bed at the good inn at Nancy, he drank a little soup. Longchamp, who had never left him for a moment all this time, ordered his own supper to be sent up to his master's room. When Voltaire had seen him put down an entrée, half a shoulder of mutton, two roast thrushes and a dozen robins, he suddenly felt hungry himself. He ate some robins and drank a little wine in his water. He then went into a sound sleep, only waking up at three the next afternoon.

To distract us from the slight nausea brought on by the thought of robins being a suitable invalid diet, let us turn to Richard Holmes who, in his *Footsteps*, retraced a few years ago Robert Louis Stevenson's famous journey through the Cévennes. In need of food and a bed, Holmes called at the La Trappe monastery and those who imagine that monks live mainly on bread and water and the word of God will have to revise their ideas.

'You are hungry, my friend,' Father Ambrose cut into my thought, 'so come with me.' And he gave me another of those Trappist smiles.

I was whisked away without ceremony to the kitchens, and sat down at a huge wooden table. Behind me, a large electric dish-washer turned like a Buddhist prayer-wheel. All round, tiles gleamed and scoured pots bubbled on brand-new gas ranges. The kitchen monk in a pressed white apron considered me thoughtfully. 'One must feed the corpse as well as the spirit,' he observed in a heavy Provençal accent, and grinned seraphically. . . . He disappeared into an echoing pantry and came out with plate after plate balanced on his arm. I could not believe such a feast, and later listed it all in my diary: dish of olives, black and green; earthern bowl of country pâté with wooden scoop; whole pink ham on the bone, with carving knife; plate of melon slices; bowl of hot garlic sausage and mash; bowl of salad and radishes; board of goats' cheeses; basket of different breads; canister of home-made butter; two jugs of wine, one white, one red. *Spécialité de la maison*, thin slices of fresh *baguette* spread very thickly with a heavy honey-coloured paste which turned out to be pounded chestnuts, *marrons*, and tasted out of this world. I was told simply: '*Mangez, mais mangez tout ce que vous voudrez!*' And he was right; I had the hunger of the devil.

The Rolland sisters did not go to such lengths to satisfy my hunger, but their splendid and varied cuisine taught me what to expect on future trips to France. On the whole, I have not been disappointed.

INDIAN SUMMER

I suppose that if you're going, fairly late in life, to surge up again from the depths of relative obscurity ('Good Lord, I thought he was dead!'), the age of sixty-five is as good as any in which to pop up your periscope once more, provided that you don't surge too vigorously, as I seem to have done, and lose your state pension. It seems that if you choose to work hard and get adequately paid for it, the government punishes you by not allowing you the pension available to men at sixty-five and for which you have been paying in for a great deal of your working life. I take it that this procedure seems fair play to somebody.

One evening, a few days before the Christmas of 1975 and just when I was wondering whether the spuds were done or not (if ever I write a cookery book, it will be called *You Can't Hurry Potatoes*), the telephone rang. It was Anthony Howard, then editor of the *New Statesman*, to say that Auberon Waugh, their Somerset correspondent, had been enticed away by the *Spectator* (though whether by its money or its views on life was not divulged) and would I therefore take over the 'First Person' column? My answer was required by the next morning. I asked how soon the first piece would be needed. 'In a fortnight.' Could the piece be, I asked, clutching at straws, about pantomimes? 'Certainly. Excellent idea.' Could I not alternate with another writer and do a piece every other week? 'No. People buy papers and magazines hoping to find, day by day and week by week, the same features in the same places.' And so next morning I accepted, comforting myself with the thought that I would take on this alarming stint for three months or so and then hand over to somebody far better fitted than I for a weekly *causerie* of 1,150 words (it was later increased to 1,400).

I was given a free hand and Tony Howard, though my politics (and I am so far to the right as to be out of sight) must have horrified him, was charmingly encouraging from the start. I realised at once that, for good or bad, readers must know something of one's life and background. I had been writing book reviews for the *New Statesman* for forty years but they are rather impersonal things. For a regular column, a more personal acquaintance is necessary (like Godfrey Winn, I kept trying not to tell myself, and that house and that dog and that mother). I therefore wrote much about my childhood and my education (rum prep school, then Oundle, and then blessed Cambridge), my keen theatre-going, and Devon, where I live. For obvious reasons and remembering charabanc-loads of fan readers in the '30s peering through the vastly more popular Beverley Nichols' hedge in an attempt to see him walking up, or down, the garden path, I disguised both my house and the village as 'Myrtlebank' and 'Appleton', but my Cousin Madge is, happily, real, as are other Devon residents, though they would hardly recognise themselves (people, apart from Hugh Walpole on that famous *Cakes and Ale* occasion, seldom do). And I have to confess that, once the initial fright had worn off, I enjoyed writing each piece, but only, as writers will know, after I had completed it and had sat back.

I rewrite a great deal, or rather, I add on. A thinnish sentence to begin with which then sprouts adjectives and clauses and adverbs and things in brackets (heaps of things in brackets). This results in long and unwieldy sentences, but never mind. And so, in January, 1976, I set to and churned out piece after piece, imagining that that would be that. But I was wrong.

Quite soon a lot of other things started to happen. Letters

for instance, and in increasing numbers. Kind letters thanking me for pleasure given. Serious letters asking whether, when I mentioned, say, Mark Twain, I had done so because I saw in his political attitudes, such as they were, a foretaste of American etc etc (I never liked to answer that I had brought him in merely because I couldn't think what on earth to write next). Letters wanting something — requests to speak at debates (Oxbridge, believe it or not), to address literary clubs, to open fêtes, to head discussions, to write prefaces for books, and to speak (and how frightening) at large London dinners. Some of these invitations, and largely the worthier ones (if that doesn't sound too smug and patronising) I accepted ('My wife will meet the 4.15 and I need hardly say how greatly we all . . . etc'). I doubt if my nice hosts, to whose societies I was to 'speak', ever realised the preparatory work involved. The view seems to be widely held that, if you can wield a pen professionally, you can also speak with ease and fluency and that you only have to open your mouth for a torrent of words to flow forth and for the necessary number of minutes (' . . . and now I see that my time is up'). This, as most of us know to our cost, is twaddle.

And one literary matter, given an impetus by my seemingly relentless rush of words in the *New Statesman*, has led to another. Two years later I started to do a fortnightly piece in the *Sunday Telegraph*, my first brush with a really wide reading public (five million, they think) and there I write on lightish (what else?) subjects kindly suggested to me by their fertile features staff. Then there have been the *Evening Standard, In Britain, Good Housekeeping*, the new smarty-boots *Tatler*, and so on. Please do not think that I mention these titles in a vain and bragging manner. I mention them merely to show that, if you never say 'No' to an offer (and I have never dared) things can develop along busy lines.

I first began broadcasting in 1934 and here again I found, at the age of sixty-five, a sudden upsurge of interest — requests to review paperbacks, live, on Radio Four, to celebrate St

George's Day on *Woman's Hour*, to do *Quote . . . Unquote* (a basically literary programme that is astonishingly popular with a very wide public), to be on *Any Questions?* where fortunately I have secured for myself the position of light-hearted waffler and firm non-answerer of the questions. And there has been a lot of telly too, if you'll forgive this self-advertisement, with Robert Robinson's *Book Programme* (I did a moving, to me, talk about Dr Watson's last years — arthritic and married to Mrs Hudson, the Baker Street landlady), Melvyn Bragg's *ditto*, *Call My Bluff* and what some would regard as the Second and First XI Colours of the television world — appearances on the *Russell Harty* and *Michael Parkinson Shows*.

I truly only mention all that to indicate how oddly things work out. It is all to me, as in *The King and I*, 'a puzzlement'. I have no special gifts. I like to think that I take a little trouble with the sentences to get them running nicely but that is all. I am rather a numbskull. I am a low-brow. I hate heavy literary discussions. I wince at the mere mention of Proust. But years ago, Somerset Maugham wrote a short story (can it have been called *Jane*?) about a woman who earned an undeserved reputation for wit by simply telling the truth. It was so unusual in life that people thought it funny. This may be what I have stumbled on. I don't prevaricate much or dress things or myself up to be what they are not. If asked whether I like Shakespeare, I give the correct answer. Not very much. There now!

THEATRELAND

ALONG THE ROUTE

For a stage-struck child, to be born in the pleasant village of Barnes was very heaven, for Barnes lay within easy bus-reach of the West End and Theatreland and that, I freely confess, was and is the London I love. And so, in addition to the rural amenities then available in SW 13 (summer walks near the Thames through fields ablaze with wild flowers and where St Paul's School now stands), you were within walking distance of the first theatre I ever went to, the King's Theatre, Hammersmith.

To get to Hammersmith, you passed, of course, over that splendid suspension bridge from where we used to watch the Boat Race, decked out with light blue ribbons and cheering wildly. On one occasion, my grandmother dropped, in her excitement, her rolled umbrella into the river. It shot straight down like a falling arrow and embedded itself in mud, whence it was retrieved at low tide by a friendly boatman (two shillings and six pence tip).

The first performance I ever went to at Hammersmith was the Christmas pantomime, *Sinbad the Sailor*. Atmospheric conditions put our presence there at risk for there was a dense pea-souper London fog, no buses or taxis were venturing forth and we had to set out on foot, my father striding ahead with a storm lantern down that road quaintly called Castelnau (after, one assumes, some Frog general who had, for once, won a battle).

Fogs were far more agreeable and romantic in fiction — Dickens and the Sherlock Holmes stories — than in fact and, as we trudged along, my coughing indicated that I was 'sickening' for something. I managed to hold out (it was measles) until *Sinbad* was over and we had shrieked for the last time at Sinbad's raffish mother, the 'dame', with her voluminous underwear constantly on view as she repeatedly ('Drat them bollards!') fell over. By then it was First World War time, and when Sinbad (a beefy girl, though one didn't realise it at the time) gave us 'There's a Long Long Trail A-Winding', there wasn't a dry eye in the house.

The surface of Castelnau, as was then the case in many of London's streets, was composed of wooden blocks, each about brick size and fitted together as snugly as a jigsaw, then covered in tarmac. This made for reduced traffic noise but created a hazard for, in torrential rain, water often seeped beneath and the wooden blocks became disjointed and started to float, a merry sight for anybody who didn't happen to want to travel.

I went to my first school, the wonderful Froebel Institute, remembered gratefully by so many, in West Kensington, and its windows looked out on the original St Paul's playing-fields, an added attraction. To get to the Froebel you had to pass the King's Theatre and so I always knew what was on (London successes frequently wound up there for a week) and could therefore pester my parents. In this way I was taken to see *The Only Way*, with Martin Harvey, and *The Scarlet Pimpernel*, with Fred Terry (uncle of Sir John Gielgud) and his wife, Julia Neilson. And one wonderful fortnight, when the Gilbert and Sullivan company were there, we went four times and I had my first of many glimpses of Henry Lytton and Bertha Lewis.

The bus that took me to school, the number nine, was to me a magical vehicle for I knew that, after dumping me, it went on to Piccadilly and thence to the Strand and Aldwych and passed on the way six theatres. Even before it got to Piccadilly there were excitements, with Mudie's Library in High Street, Kensington, and on the right a shop called Pontings, and then Derry and Toms with its thrilling roof garden (a real fountain playing!) and Barkers, whose Food Halls had such a remarkably distinct and attractive smell.

And then there were Kensington Gardens and the Albert Hall ('Next Week: *Hiawatha* with a chorus of eighty') and Knightsbridge Barracks where, if your luck was in, you got a peep at the Household Cavalry returning home. Excitement rose as Green Park and the Ritz came into view, and before long you could see the façade of the London Pavilion and the electric bulbs announcing what was playing there (*On With The Dance*, with Delysia).

Seated in the bus, and in the prime position (in front and on top, unless it was raining, for there were then no roofs to buses), I kept my eyes glued to the people passing on the pavement in case I could spot an actor or actress. I knew practically all of them by sight from photographs in magazines and newspapers, and in this way I saw a great star, Leslie Faber, in the Haymarket, and dear Mary Brough, of the famous Aldwych farces, in the Strand. And Jack Buchanan and Dorothy Dickson in Piccadilly. And once I saw somebody I was nearly certain was Gladys Cooper, coming out of the Carlton Hotel.

At that time, a popular and relatively cheap way of seeing a matinee was to queue for the pit and this my mother and I constantly did. Once when we were queuing for a sensational play called *Interference* at the St James's in King Street, now alas no more, the star of the piece, Gerald du Maurier came by and smiled charmingly. And once, after a performance of *A Safety Match* at the Strand, my mother found that she had left her bag in the theatre and we had to go in again and fetch it. We found the curtain up and the scenery being stacked to one side of the stage. That was a day and a half, I can tell you!

Although some of the theatres have vanished, and the National Theatre has as yet no atmosphere, and I don't nowadays always like what I see on stages, I know that, if I were to take that number nine bus again, the old excitement would return, though stars are proper stars no more and it

would be ghosts that I would see upon the pavements —
Yvonne Arnaud, perhaps, and Tom Walls looking jaunty,
and dear Cicely Courtneidge chuckling, and Marie Tempest
in a pretty hat.

TEA FOR TWO

I do not wish to seem to boast in any way but I suppose that I must now be one of the very few persons left in the country who could sing for you, *in French*, the title song of the musical comedy *No, No, Nanette*.

Nanette was, you'll recall, a very pretty girl (in 1925 at the Palace she was the entrancing Binnie Hale) whose simple whims — a bicycle ride, a game of ping-pong — were for ever being thwarted, the men's chorus, twenty-strong, wagging their fingers reprovingly at her and all going 'NO!'

I could also do for you the big hit number, Tea for Two, and by way of proof;

> Picture you
> Upon my knee,
> Just tea for two
> And two for tea.

comes out as

> Je vous vois
> Déjà chez nous,
> Buvant du thé
> Sur mes genoux.

For the benefit of those who have no smattering of the lingo, *buvant* means drinking, *thé* is tea and *genoux* are knees (note the interesting plural ending in -x, a distinction which it shares with *poux* or lice).

But how, you wonder, did this enviable vocal ability

become mine? And how indeed did a head already so richly stocked with valuable data not only find room for these pleasing lyrics but also have the power to retain them down the years?

My chance came while I was a student in 1928 at Grenoble University. By day we studied the plays of somebody called Racine. If his plays haven't yet come your way, try to let it stay like that. If Racine knew any jokes, he kept them to himself. The plays are full of ladies with very fancy names getting into emotional muddles in verse. One longed for Andromaque (yes, she was one of them) to come rushing on looking fussed and saying that the downstairs WC had got itself blocked and could anybody remember the plumber's number. But no such luck.

When evening came in Grenoble I longed for lighter dramatic fare and fortunately there arrived at the theatre a French touring company of *No, No, Nanette*, the piece being fully recognisable under its French name (they had decided on *Non, Non, Nanette*). To get Racine fully out of my system, I went night after night, applauding loudly and requesting encores. The French, perverse as ever, do not use the word *encore* for 'encore'. They just curtly shout 'twice', which comes out as *bis*. I ask you! (*Je vous demande!*)

Oldsters like myself will have been delighted to note a recent spate of musical comedy revivals, with *Oh, Kay!* at Chichester, the triumphant London run of *Mr Cinders* and, only a few years ago, Nanette herself at Drury Lane. And now we have *On Your Toes* and the affectionate pastiche, *The Boy Friend*. One lives in hopes of *Mercenary Mary*, a veritable treasure-chest of tuneful liveliness.

It is too much to expect that future revivals will attempt to reproduce the original scenery. The last act usually took place on a sun-drenched terrace by the sea overhung by giant wistaria blossoms attached to netting. On the right there was part of a house with a french window wide enough to permit twenty-four chorus girls to come hopping through on one leg and with the other leg held high above their heads. The programme showed them to be 'Guests at Frouville-sur-Mer'.

And the jokes! Oh how merry they were! For many years now I have been a devotee of The Joke That Seemed Funny At The Time. *Punch* of course led the way with the curate's egg, and let me remind you of two more—I give the pay-off line in brackets. 'You can always tell a Kensington girl' ('Yes, but you cannot tell her much'). 'I'm a little stiff from badminton' ('I don't care where you're from').

There was a jolly moment in *Blue Eyes* (1928) when the soubrette, boasting of what I suppose people would now refer to as her 'personal freshness', said: 'I always put violet in my bath,' upon which her gentleman friend came back with the witty riposte: 'I would do the same if only I knew Violet.' They then burst loudly into song.

Care to hear the opening chorus of Jack Buchanan's *That's A Good Girl*? I'm ready when you are.

PURSE THE LIPS

Random thoughts frequently come, unbidden, to my mind and at moments when I am usually busily occupied at some domestic task that bears no relation at all to the *pensée* that arrives. How and why one's brain, for such I defiantly call it, manages these matters is to me one of the eternal mysteries. Thus, only the other day and after I had just decided that the cleanliness of my newest Marks and Spencer shirt (size sixteen and a half and in a rather pleasing Cambridge blue) fully warranted another day's wear before I need wash and drip-dry it, an interesting thought popped up from nowhere. I had turned aside a moment from my laundry in order to construct a small fish pie, and you'll probably want to know the reason why (it comes under the 'Look Ahead' heading). Next day I had, with the help of my friendly Exeter dentist, himself possessed of fine rows of gleaming teeth and such a striking advertisement for his art, to say farewell to a dear old friend, a chipped and wobbly back molar. Fearing a subsequently sore gum and painful eating, I decided that fish was the answer. Our travelling fish man had conveniently called and just after I had cooked and flaked my fish (a generous measure of halibut), grated my cheese and was about to make a delicious white and cheesy and milky *roux* to combine with the fish (and do please feel free to copy this recipe if it has set you salivating), it occurred to me to wonder how many years it has been since anybody, and ladies particularly, whistled in a music-hall.

Do not misunderstand me. I am not here referring to those

44

vulgar and piercing noises made by some audiences and almost all football crowds (the Italians are especially good at it; it would seem to be, currently, their most outstanding contribution to life), but to the music-hall item that announced itself as being a *siffleur* or, more usually, a *siffleuse*. But why, you ask, use a Frog word? The reason is that, with any serious musical item in music-halls, taste and refinement were considered to be essential (those trios of piano, violin and 'cello always performed with draped curtains of apricot silk behind them, and a standard lamp with gold tassels) and there is no doubt that the word *siffleuse* contains a good bit more taste and refinement than 'Whistling Woman', the latter calling to mind some drawing, perhaps by Belcher, whose talents many will remember with pleasure, of a buxom Billingsgate lady going merrily about her fishy tasks and greeting the morning with a few gladsome whistles.

As, from about the age of five, my every waking thought that did not concern food was directed towards theatres and music-halls and the, to me, enchanted persons who appeared in them, I knew exactly what a *siffleuse* was and did, and one thrilling day my mother, ever ready to provide a joyous surprise and who never failed to back me up and encourage my theatrical leanings, said that we were going to have lunch with an old acquaintance, a lady who was, and I forget now which, either the widow or sister or cousin or aunt of 'Athel Capper, the *siffleur*'. This is now about sixty years ago and I may well have misremembered the Christian name, but of Capper I am sure. My mother, pressed for details as to where and what he had whistled, could, alas, recall no more. Our hostess, whom I will call Mrs Capper, lived in a charming eighteenth-century house easily accessible (and it still stands) from, of all places, the GWR station at Aldermaston. Nobody marched in those days to Aldermaston, an atom was something that merely occurred in conversation ('it's not an atom of use') and the countryside was unspoilt.

My excitement, as so often in youth, knew no bounds.

Although she was, obviously, not Mr Capper, would Mrs Capper come bounding in and make an entrance, perhaps to a fanfare? Would she have made herself heavily up? Would she wear a dress that glittered? Would she too, perhaps, whistle? She did, regretfully, none of these things. She was just a pleasant and white-haired lady who gave us a delicious lunch and talked of matters that did not, and oh, the disappointment, in any way concern music-halls or whistling. I looked about for happy snaps of fellow artistes (Vesta Tiller, perhaps, or Harry Lauder), signed with a flourish, encased in silver frames and, probably, gracing the Bechstein. None were visible, and one could only assume that our hostess's relationship with the *siffleur* must have been a pretty distant one — second cousin-by-marriage, possibly. Still, lunch had been agreeable, the railway trip had been interesting (I had only been sick once, at Reading West) and even such a very slight brush with the world of entertainment had been better than none.

But, and in the strange way that things happen, I did once positively meet and stand next to an actual working *siffleuse* just before and after she had been in full vocal action and delighting her public. By profession, my father was an electrical engineer, which means an engineer who specialises in electrical matters rather than one who is worked by electricity, and it was suddenly discovered, in about 1917, that one of the men who had worked for him was now chief electrician at a music-hall which stood to the west of Hammersmith and was called the Chiswick Empire, conveniently close to Barnes, where we lived. Strings were pulled and permission was kindly given by the management for me to be present, back-stage and at the First House (6.15) during a performance. None of life's major excitements and pleasures (and I have no intention of providing my list of them: *chacun a son goût*) could possibly compare with what I then felt.

My stomach, ever in youth something to be reckoned with, was calmed and fortified with buttered toast and a boiled egg at tea-time and off we set (my father was to accompany me backstage, while my mother was placed in a front stall). In a daze, we passed through the stage-door and, for me, a delirium of delight began. Wonderful theatre smells to begin with, that weird and fusty musty mixture of canvas, wood, sweat, size, paint and clothes. Then there was the feeling of dedication, and an air of expectancy everywhere. The half-light in the wings and the glimpses of the bright stage. The orchestra playing, the performers at work, the whispers ('Stand just there and don't make a sound'). They very sportingly stationed me right down stage in the prompt corner and when, in the interval, the safety curtain came down, it almost took my nose off. For the second half I was put in the flies, climbing there up a steep ladder, with my father behind me in case I fell, and enjoying up there the fascinating sight of the backdrops and curtain being hauled up and down and, peering down onto the stage, watching a man and woman giving a splendid imitation of Gaby Deslys and her dancing partner, Harry Pilcer, great stars and all the rage.

The second item on the programme, and coloured lights on the sides of the proscenium showed which number we had got to, was a *siffleuse*. To get the thing away to a good start, we had kicked off with a comical trick cyclist, red-nosed to indicate insobriety, who, by pretending to be about to bicycle straight into the audience, had managed to put them into an exceptionally happy mood. During his turn, I had become aware of, waiting near me, a slim presence dressed in a black and glittering substance. It was our *siffleuse*, and she looked nervous. It was my first realisation of the fact that almost all performers everywhere are always nervous (and if they aren't, there is something gravely wrong). The trick cyclist finished and took two bows, the orchestra struck up something operatic and demandingly coloratura and our *siffleuse*, inflating her lungs, glided on stage whistling violently. There was more to her art than mere whistling. In addition to keeping the expression pleasant, she had to time her slow walk across the stage so that she ended her warblings at the very moment when she exited the other side. She managed it perfectly and then reappeared, to storms of applause, and returned to my side of the stage with 'Roses of Picardy' which, being only an encore number, was somewhat shorter and required a slightly brisker progress. She came off, saw me goggling excitedly at her, said something warm and friendly, and disappeared. She had helped to give me one of the most enthralling evenings I have ever known, and I do very much hope that Life was kind to her.

WHAT'S ON (1925)

Chatting on the subject here and there and now and again down the years to my fellow residents of the delightful Devon village of Appleton, I have discovered that not one of them has ever been what is known as a really ardent theatre-goer. Geography is partly responsible. To have been such a one, it is really necessary to have lived in, or to have been within easy striking distance of, London.

Visits long ago sometimes included a theatre. Miss Entwhistle is nearly certain that she saw, during the First World War, *Chu Chin Chow*, but on the other hand she thinks that it may well have been *The Maid of the Mountains*. 'Was there a camel in it?' I asked, hot for certainties. 'Or, failing a camel, was there José Collins?' Alas, the mists of memory have closed round this exciting evening, obviously the high spot of Miss Entwhistle's dramatic experience. Pressed further, her information that the piece contained much tuneful music gets us nowhere, and since then her theatrical outings have been confined to visits to the wholly excellent 'Fol-De-Rol' concert parties (you could, as they say, take your aunt) when they used to come and brighten Torquay summers. But elsewhere I have found more accurate memories. Canon and Mrs Mountjoy were quite adventuresome. The Canon went, as a boy, to *The Farmer's Wife* ('I *roared*!') and on the evening of the day that they became engaged, the happy pair took in a merry musical called *Going Greek* ('We *shrieked*!'). And my Cousin Madge, London-based for part of her life, can still quote some large and rib-tickling sections of *Tonight's The Night* and possesses

several dear old 78s of *Glamorous Night*. None of this, however, adds up to a truly devoted reverence for our
stage.

My friends the Bultitudes certainly outdo everybody else in
the actual number of theatre visits made, being still inclined
to, in their own phrase, 'crash up to Town and do a show'.
Giles has in the past favoured what he still longingly refers to
as 'leg shows' (the tired businessman, exhausted after a day
spent cornering jute, was said to cheer up no end when a row
of smiling chorus girls hauled up their skirts and waved their
legs at him), while Bunty, intellectually the slightly more
powerful of this charming pair, used to treat herself to such
undoubted pleasures as *Perchance to Dream* and *Worm's Eye
View*. But now, when they plan to make another thrilling dash
to London ('The Dorchester's terribly full but they've
managed to squeeze us in, bless them'), they ask me for my
advice about what would be best for them to see ('What's that
thing at the Vaudeville?'). They ask me because, as I go so
frequently to London and am faintly connected with the
entertainment world, it is locally and incorrectly assumed that
Shaftesbury Avenue is what I suppose I must now call 'my
scene'. I do not like to tell them that, when it comes to
choosing nowadays a pleasurable evening's entertainment, I
am every bit as much at a loss as they are. *Où sont les George and
Margaret d'antan?*

For one thing, I no longer know where or what many of the
advertised theatres actually are, though this matters little to
me as the chances of my ever getting to them are somewhat
small. I have heard it rumoured that they sometimes tend to
stage 'black' comedies called something like *Mind My Surgical
Boot* or, quite simply, *Filth*, during which a number of people
disrobe and insult the audiences in a variety of ways. They
must be out to shock, though it is not the shock I would resent
but the boredom. But among newish theatres, I have certainly
passed, on a bus, the National, which was to me a very
cheering sight, bearing as it does to my eyes a strong

resemblance to the Newton Abbot multi-storey car park, scene of many a triumphant shopping expedition ('My *dear*, Macfisheries have got mussels!'). I have not yet dared to venture inside though I have enjoyed some offerings that have eventually crossed the water and have been put on for a run in the recognisable and commercial theatres that I have long known and loved. But after the experience of A.J.P Taylor (didn't he lose his way out and find himself upon the roof, unable to descend?) I can hardly send the Bultitudes to the National, and, if not, where? What would provide them with a novel and a happy evening?

In, say, 1925 there would have been no problem, so abundant would the Bultitude possibilities have been. It was in the theatre a merry mad vintage time for low brows, among whom I most happily count myself. For some reason, almost anything set elsewhere than in England was immensely popular. Thus, in *Fata Morgana* at the Criterion, Jeanne de Casalis (later to be the wireless's deliciously dithering 'Mrs Feather') was to be seen on what the programme described as 'the great Hungarian plain known as the Puszta' (pronounced, I can only suppose, 'pushed her') busily seducing an attractive young anchorite. (Upper Circle, five shillings and nine-pence.) Miss de Casalis's seduction kit consisted of an apricot satin house-gown with generously slashed skirt and gleaming court shoes in a silvery pattern. From her dress there hung, here and there, a heavy tassel or two, and the length of time that she required was approximately fifty minutes. The gentleman on the receiving end was a young American actor of considerable charm called Tom Douglas, though how or why he had ever got to the great Hungarian plain known as the Puszta was never explained. Endless playgoers, signing themselves 'Horrified Stall-ite', wrote in to say how revolted they had been (the then Bishop of London was being constantly revolted) and business at the box office was pleasingly brisk.

Well then, at the Playhouse, a theatre which was to be

51

closely associated (remember *The Letter*?) with that stunningly English beauty, Gladys Cooper, some very un-English activities were going on and Horrified Stall-ites were pressing in to see something described as 'a play of the primitive in three Acts'. It was called *White Cargo* and it showed a dusky and semi-clad half-caste siren called Tondelayo (she always sounded to me rather like a particularly cheerful kind of yodel) encouraging mammy palaver among white men sweatily marooned in an African outpost of Empire. Excitement ran high, and not only on the stage. The Lord Chamberlain, interfering old donkey, insisted that Tondelayo should, in spite of the sultry weather, put on more clothes (one feels that he would have liked to see her in a tweed costume and one of those tweed hats with a feather in it). Then one of the many touring companies found its theatre posters seized by the police at South Shields (acting-manager severely reprimanded). Meanwhile there was a fine fuss about the play being pirated from a novel called *Hell's Playground*. And through it all, Tondelayo continued to drive them all mad among the mangrove swamps. (Standing Room, three shillings.) This, I feel, would have been rather the thing for Giles Bultitude to have seen on the quiet while Bunty was away, kindly visiting a sick aunt at Weybridge.

My own favourite treat of 1925 was without doubt a musical called *Katja the Dancer* (it moved to Daly's from the Gaiety), for which we were somewhere in the mysterious Balkans and in the classy world of Count Orpitch and Prince Carl of Koruja (the hero, you know) and it required the heroine, tuneful Lilian Davies, to close Act Two by fainting sensationally backwards (I forget quite why) with a cry of 'Carl!' down a flight of at least four stairs (it may well have been five). Our hands were quite raw with clapping. But, though sensational faints are well enough, what we were really waiting for was for an entrancing soubrette called Ivy Tresmand and a very jolly light comedian, Gene Gerrard, to sing the great hit of the evening, a popular song called 'Leander', the Christian name of the role played by Mr Gerrard. Determined as I am to bring you part of the lyrics, I have to strain my memory back fifty-four years, so pray bear with me:

> With your Leander, your old goosey-gander,
> Far off you will wander, by land or by sea.
> Off we'll meander, for nothing could be grander
> > Than life as the wife
> > Of a bloke as broke as he.

The song never had fewer than six 'encore' choruses, in which almost everything, as you will have twigged, rhymed cleverly with Leander. (Matinees Wed and Sat.)

Down memory's lane, other delights of 1925 come flooding. At Drury Lane there was *Rose Marie*, the plot activated by yet another half-caste adventuress with eyes on the hero ('You come to Wanda's cabin, maybe?' she hissed at him, undulating a little, towards the end of Act One while the vast orchestra scraped dramatic chords in a minor key). The Aldwych farces were in fullest swing with *A Cuckoo in the Nest* (how splendid that such pieces are now being revived), with Yvonne Arnaud squeaking away in the Frog accent that she was so careful to preserve and, even, improve, Tom Walls as a pickled Major and Robertson Hare as, of course, a curate. And for the enjoyment, I hope, of some of our older readers, with their own joyous recollections ('It was our binge for Mona's twenty-first and we took a box'), I add a mere list of titles: *No, No, Nanette!*, *The Vortex*, *Charlot's Revue* (Miss Lillie, Miss Lawrence, Mr Buchanan), *The Green Hat*, *Hay Fever*, *The CoOptimists* and *On With the Dance*. Goodness me; my eyes mist over at the very names.

DON'T DILLY DALLY

Those of us who have been worrying ourselves into fiddle-strings over the disintegrating Skylab above our heads must still go right on worrying. We who have been diligently praying to the Almighty for further information, preferably of a reassuring kind, about this peril from the skies have been vouchsafed a direct answer to prayer. Those who pray regularly will know only too well that by no means all answers to prayer are agreeable and this one is no exception, though it does start off in a misleadingly cheering manner. A delightful American reader from the New York area has sent me a cutting from her newspaper to the effect that a group of Washington computer experts have put their heads and their computers together and, quaintly calling themselves Chicken Little Associates, are going to make continuous computer estimates as to exactly where Skylab, the National Aeronautics and Space Administration's orbiting laboratory that is now superfluous to requirements, is going to descend in dangerous smithereens to earth.

Restrain at once your sighs of relief. There is little here for your comfort. First of all, to register as a recipient of the latest computer gen you have to stump up the equivalent of fifty pounds a month in order to get news of the 'risk pattern' and the likelihood of the contraption zooming lethally down in your vicinity. The satellite's orbit has been, in the technical term, 'decaying' rapidly and the shower of metallic wreckage may be expected to arrive 'some time between July and September' and ideally timed to ruin everybody's hols. As the

54

Skylab's orbits cover the entire earth between fifty degrees north and fifty degrees south, most of the world's major cities are theoretically in its range. At the very most, an hour's warning may be expected. And, even with those computers whirring round, it is plain that nobody has the faintest idea of what is going to happen. Personally, I'm hanging on to my fifty pounds.

So much for experts. It is the old old story when we are hot for certainties — 'No one can tell me. Nobody knows.' A quotation from where, you ask yourself? Theatre buffs should be pricking up their ears for it comes from the land of paint and powder. It was in a pleasing little 'encore' number in a revue of the 1920s, wistfully sung by the highly talented thistledown *danseuse* and vocalist called Mimi Crawford, as pretty as a picture and much in theatrical demand (she exists, alas, no more). It was not of course to the exact position of the Skylab that Miss Crawford was here referring but to the wind. 'No one can tell me. Nobody knows,' she sang, 'where the wind comes from, where the wind goes.' Not strictly accurate, perhaps, as the origin and destination of some winds are woefully and noisily clear, but the number's general message is obvious to all and it gave Miss Crawford, the singing once over, a chance to twiddle and twirl most charmingly. She married an Earl (an extremely brave wartime UXB victim) and became the Countess of Suffolk.

She did more besides. When, a number of months ago, I wrote about Goethe's poor old mother and bewailed the fact that so few people could in the last few years have been thinking of the dear soul and how distressing a retreat into such total obscurity was, I got a letter from a lady in Reading to say that, as it happens, she had been thinking of Frau Goethe 'only this morning', though what had sparked off this fruitful train of thought she did not mention. There are much better grounds for remembering Miss Crawford for it was she who sang, in the revue *Many Happy Returns* at the Duke of York's in 1928, the number whose chorus went 'I've danced with a man who's danced with a girl who's danced with the Prince of Wales,' the song which formed such a feature of that fine *Edward and Mrs Simpson* ITV series. The lyrics made originally something of a stir as they were thought to be in pretty bad taste. Written by the superbly gifted Herbert Farjeon, the song's verse began merrily with 'My word I've had a party, my word I've had a spree,' but it was frostily received on the first night, attacked by the *Daily Mail* and, even though the Prince graciously stated that he had no objections, the number was subsequently withdrawn from the revue, the 'Theatre World' magazine clicking its tongue in dismay and announcing its stupefaction, a feeling shared by many of the rest of us, that 'this infectious little song, so daintily rendered by Miss Crawford, could possibly annoy anybody'.

Such fastidiousness about the possible hurting of royal feelings did not always obtain in the last century. Queen Victoria, hearing a catchy tune being played by a military band on the terrace at Windsor, sent to enquire what the title of it might be and had to be informed that the piece was called 'Come Where the Booze is Cheaper'. In the song 'Burlington Bertie from Bow', a very popular number invariably performed by male impersonators such as Ella Shields and Hetty King, there was, if memory serves, a line which went 'The Prince of Wales' brother says come and meet mother', which conjured up a delightful picture of a cosy Palace *tête-à-tête* between the queen and this down-at-heel man-about-town, bravely struggling to keep up appearances in reduced circumstances and collecting his cigar ends from the Strand's gutters. And despite the existence of songs such as 'Send for Mother, Birdie's Dying' and 'Ring the Bell Softly, There's Crêpe on the Door', a tremendous jolliness was everywhere in the entertainment world, as Patrick Beaver splendidly reminds us in *The Spice of Life*, an excellent review of the assorted pleasures of the Victorian age.

However disagreeable life must have been for many, the

Victorians, rich and poor, at least knew how to enjoy themselves. Every town of even modest size had its music-hall, its fair and regular visits from tenting circuses. Theatres all over the country were filled with touring companies. Above all there was the pantomime (at Christmas in 1853 central London boasted no fewer than fourteen), with Widow Twankey, although resident in 'ancient Peking', making her first entrance riding a wobbly bicycle, and comic royalties called King Hupsydown and King Wrongsydeup and a text so peppered with merry puns (always italicised in print so that nobody can possibly miss the fun) that we find the Peking *blanchisseuse* bewailing her housekeeping deficiencies with

> Like the receptacle of Mrs Hubbard,
> No food can in *dis cupboard* be *discubbard*.

But it was in the music-hall, where the subjects sung about were the real basics of life — kippers, drunkenness, patriotism, mothers-in-law, policemen, lodgers, children, infidelity, the seaside, brawls, rent arrears — where the gaiety positively bubbled forth. Assorted titles, sentimental, comical and indecent, tell the whole happy story — 'Boiled Beef and Carrots', 'A Little Bit of Cucumber', Captain Ginjah ('I like the ladies, not one of them would I injah'), 'Hit Him on the Boko' ('Dot him on the snitch'), 'The Bower that Stands in Thigh Lane', 'Shall I be an Angel, Daddy?', 'Stand Me a Cab-fare, Duckie', 'The Baby's Name is Kitchener', and so on. One has, of course, one's favourite moment. This for me was in a Billie Merson number called 'The Night I Appeared as Macbeth' and which contained the following:

> I acted so tragic
> The house rose like magic
> The audience cried 'You're sublime';
> They made me a present
> Of Mornington Crescent,
> They threw it a brick at a time.

THE STORY AND THE SONG

Once the British have decided that one of their many favourite characters, be he or she famous in history's pages or with the pen or the brush or in the world of entertainment, is supreme and beyond reproach and have placed him or her firmly upon a pedestal, they are extremely reluctant to have their attention drawn to the fact that there are some worrying cracks further down the plinth.

A bold statement that Churchill was, in some ways and to put it mildly, a bit of a pickle and what used to be called 'a holy terror', would net me such a shoal of abusive letters that therefore I will not make it. Similarly, if I were to say that Montgomery, though splendid in battle and born with a face that happened to fit, became in retirement a conceited ass, I might be attacked in the street or molested at 'Myrtlebank' (if they can find it) and therefore I will say no such thing. And in quite another field, if I put forward the view that the actress Marie Tempest, though entirely dazzling when she wished to be, was odious to her inferiors and a toad in the theatre who treated matinée audiences with contempt (I've caught her at it often enough), I might be stoned by the gallery first-nighters, though surely by now they must be a lapsed body of devotees, and more's the pity for they loved the theatre and kept everybody on their toes.

I have two small squabbles with two writers of distinction, to say the least of it, one of them be-pedestalled (and no pedestal is higher), and the other, alas, and to our island's discredit, for a long time out of favour and de-pedestalled. The first of these august figures is the Swan of Avon, inclined in my opinion to run on a bit and make ten words do the work of one and sometimes, when being funny, to be painful. The merry dialogue that I find so especially trying occurs in *The Merchant of Venice*, Act I Scene II where the rich and spoilt heiress, Portia, relaxing in her boudoir (I have always suspected her of having apricot satin cushions and of slopping about in mules) with her sickeningly sycophantic 'waiting-maid', Nerissa, runs over the names and alleged non-attributes of her current gentleman callers, both of the ladies going off into fits of laughter the while. I don't mind it so much when the odious girl mocks at three of her suitors — a Neapolitan prince, a local landowner and a Frenchman (named Monsieur Le Bon, of all feeble inventions) — for they are three Europeans, and foreigners must learn to take what comes, nice or nasty as the case may be. It is when she is impertinent about handsome Lord Falconbridge of England (I somehow see him with a lovely 'place' near East Grinstead) and complains that he cannot speak Italian (and what proper, red-blooded Englishman would even wish to, may I ask?) that I get ratty. She is then jocular at the expense of a Scottish lord, kilts and all. Not a girl to encourage in any way whatsoever.

The second writer is one with whom I have communication almost every day of my life. When at home, I would not dream of closing my eyes in sleep without reading at least two paragraphs of his masterly works. Soothing. It is not, as though I need to point this out, that he is in any way soporific. It is more in the comforting spirit that, if I were to die unexpectedly in the night, one's eyes would, at least, have looked last on greatness. Some there are who read, before clicking out the light, the Bible, and extremely unsettling and nightmarish a lot of it must be. I read P.G. Wodehouse. I do not, unfortunately, own the complete canon or anything like it (getting on for ninety books, I believe), but I have, I suppose, about fifty of them, including the indispensable Mulliner and Jeeves omnibuses, and it is enough to enable me to ring the changes. Not that it is changes that I always want. I must, I suppose, have read the long short story *The Crime Wave at Blandings* upwards of two hundred times and there are sentences that, even though I know well enough that they are coming, still give me a sharp stab of delight. For example, that moment when Lord Emsworth's forbidding sister, Lady Constance Keeble, informs him that his grandson, George, has just shot the irritating secretary, Rupert Baxter, with an airgun. ' "Good!" cried Lord Emsworth, then prudently added the word "gracious." '

It is not, Heaven help me, with the impeccable prose, the riotously funny characters or the marvellously complicated plots that my little difference lies but with Wodehouse's reputation as a writer of lyrics for the musical comedies with which he occupied himself for so many successful years. He is, I state, conscious of a feeling of disloyalty and ingratitude, no lyric writer. The lyric most commonly mentioned, and frequently in terms of awe and veneration and wonderment, is from the musical play *Show Boat* and is for a song called 'Bill' with an enchanting Kern tune and sung in London at Drury Lane by Marie Burke as Julie. The charm of the character Bill was that he was such an ordinary man and to make this crystal clear, Wodehouse supplied a verse which includes the lines,

> He can't play golf or tennis or polo,
> Or sing a solo,
> Or row.

The chorus contains the following:

> His form and face,
> His manly grace,
> Are not the kind that you
> Would find in a statue.

I must leave you to judge.

Although he was much more involved in Broadway musicals of fifty and sixty years ago than in purely English offerings, Wodehouse gets a mention in a pleasant new book, a 'must' for all middle-aged theatre buffs of the less intellectually demanding kind and which provides a comprehensive survey of English musical plays from 1916 to 1978, and those of us who missed very few of the productions in these theatrically happy and fecund years are in for a nostalgic feast. Derek and Julia Parker are the admirable authors, joyfully enthusiastic about their subject, of *The Story and the Song*. The photographs are especially well chosen and strike vibrant chords of memory — Brian Reece as the Hon Thomas Trout in *Bless the Bride*, the no-expense-spared gypsy wedding (Ivor in profile, natch) from *Glamorous Night*, Noel, Frog accent firmly in position, as an improbable French marquis in *Conversation Piece*, José Collins (one of the three great 'theatre' voices) surrounded by whiskery bandits in *The Maid of the Mountains*, goggle-eyed Leslie Henson splendidly inebriated in *Funny Face*, and the delightful singing-lesson scene at the beginning of *Bitter-Sweet*, with the singing-master hero played by George Metaxa, not Cochran's first choice for the role but the Viennese tenor whom he wanted was called Hans Unterfucker and it was generally felt that the name 'Metaxa' would look more attractive on the billboards. There is also a happy snap from the elaborate Temple Ballet from *Careless Rapture* and showing Ivor in a natty pair of elasticated gum boots, roomy black briefs and little else, advancing meaningfully upon Miss Dorothy Dickson, herself attired in a flimsy negligee with rose-petal train and wearing in addition an expression of considerable alarm. One got one's money's worth in those days.

The Parkers have dug out some fascinating facts. In *Tonight's The Night*, the leading lady, Madge Saunders, was so sensationally beautiful that the Sultan of Zanzibar, visiting the Gaiety one evening, became so wildly enamoured of her that he informed the management that he wished to buy her. The camel in *Chu Chin Chow*, an animal about whose welfare I used to worry as a boy, was being walked round His Majesty's

Theatre one day in order to stretch its legs, or something, when it fell through a pavement-light into a cellar and was killed. The successor to this record-breaking musical was to be called *Mecca* but the Lord Chamberlain (and a truthful history of that risible office would be merry indeed) insisted that the title should be changed as the name Mecca used in this way might give offence to British Moslems. He stuck to his guns even when the management pointed out that a very popular medicament of the day was called Mecca Pills for Piles.

GOOD HEALTH

I'm sorry to say that I'm really very poorly equipped for modern life. I just don't seem to get the hang of it somehow. It's partly because I don't know the technical terms for anything. Take yachting, of which we see quite a bit on the telly. If a British boat starts to do well, I find myself saying: 'Oh look, they've pulled up some bigger sails,' only to be put instantly to shame by the commentator's smarty-boots comment: 'Ah, I see they've crowded on more canvas.' Well then, there's a lot of jaw these days about 'differentials being eroded'. Now what in heaven's name are differentials? Do *I* have any differentials? And if everybody's got differentials, who is being so beastly as to erode mine? Whoever you are, kindly take your hands off my differentials.

And modern art is another area where I miss out. You know, you go into a gallery for a peep at something soothing and you see two huge and lumpy hunks of stone standing on a plinth, one of them with a large hole through its middle, and you find that the ensemble is valued at £84,000 and calls itself *Ecstasy*. Or perhaps it's an action painting where the artist stands well back and lets fly with dollops of paint which land haphazardly and the result is valued at £195,000 and is called something like *Thought for a June morning* or *Bognor at Dusk*.

But it's really in the matter of clothes that I'm such a complete flop. A recent newspaper article announced that the average man possessed clothes worth £700 and which included six suits, six jackets, five pairs of bags, four pairs of jeans, eight knitwear items, two raincoats, three topcoats, and five T-shirts. All I can say when faced with this list is: 'Oh *dear*!' However, I did go the other day to what is called 'a well-known store' to buy a new sports coat, as we used to describe them. A kind assistant took one look at me, snug in my only macintosh, and, leading me to a rack of jackets, soon found me a pleasantly roomy one. I glanced at the ticket. 'Forty-four inches,' it said, 'and portly.' Portly indeed! Oh yes, I bought it. I don't mind.

ON MY SICK BED

Sometimes, when totally exhausted (as who isn't?) by Life, a wild urge comes to me to let it be known that I am ill, take to my bed for a week or so and just lie there staring, quietly and restfully, at the ceiling. Of course, as we all know, the word 'ill' worries everybody and is one that has for years been carefully avoided by the British people, who fear it and have therefore invented endless and less fussing substitutes. As it will be best in any case to leave the actual nature of my malaise very vague, I shall probably settle for saying; 'I must have been over-doing things a little.' Or perhaps I shall use: 'The doctor didn't like the look of me,' (all too true, I dare say) and my sympathetic friends can then pass on the distressing news to each other in the various words and phrases that come more easily to the lips — seedy, off colour, below par, not quite one hundred per cent, a bit under the weather, and 'not too good, I'm afraid'.

I must on no account imply that I have anything that is in any way catching. This would isolate me and would be madness for somebody who does not like to be separated from his creature comforts and those who supply them. So it must just be a bodily imperfection or weakness of some sort ('I think the old ticker needs a bit of a rest'). Neither must it be anything the slightest bit gastric and it might be as well to croak out: 'The silly part about it is that I'm *eating* very well, so that's something to be thankful for.' This, you see, will not discourage well-wishers from calling on me with assorted goodies — grapes (a bit dull these days, but well meant), canisters of nourishing soup, drop scones, home-made fudge, all nestling in tissue paper and perched up in those wicker baskets to which people's minds always fly when contemplating a visit to a bedside. Of course, if they care to throw in a bottle of whisky as well, that's up to them. It might be just the very thing for my old ticker. ('Just put it down on this little table by the bed. *How* good of you!')

In order to banish from my visitors any sneaking suspicion that I am a fraud, I possess an enormous white woolly bed-jacket that used to belong to my sadly asthmatic grandfather. A garment of this kind instantly spells 'illness'. An extra pillow or two, the bed-jacket, a carafe of fresh water, a box of tissues and a brave little smile ('How wonderful of you to keep so cheerful!') are going to fool nearly all my friends. And then and in addition, I'm all ready with: 'Sorry to be such a beastly nuisance,' followed by the slightest of coughs and much noisy pouring from the carafe. A wife would, of course, put a brisk end to such rubbish but then I have no wife and the world is very kind to bachelors living on their own. Try it some time.

My callers are likely, and bless them for it, to be mainly feminine ('Gerald's fishing') and before long one of the older ones, patting and adjusting my pillows, is going to comfort me with: 'Well, as I always say, Dr Rest is Dr Best.' If she goes on to make mention of two other medical men called Dr Diet and Dr Quiet, it will be clear to me that she possesses a copy of an invaluable Victorian volume called *Enquire Within Upon Everything*, originally published in 1856 and full of cosily-named fictitious doctors of the kind mentioned. The book deals freely with illnesses and cures but the advertisement that first brought this gem-packed tome to the attention of the public announced, in terms that some might consider boastful, that it could solve every domestic problem and would tell how to model flowers in wax, stop hiccoughs, get married, bury a relative (legally and with the help of others, I mean) and what to do for the best with somebody who has inadvertently poisoned himself with deadly nightshade and is in a coma

(smelling salts to the nostrils first, and then 'rouse by electricity', though a suitable voltage is not mentioned, nor which
are the absolutely ideal areas for applying the wires to).

Our compilers flinch at nothing that is even remotely
medical and an indication of their quality comes in their firm
way of tackling insomnia. Sleeplessness is entirely due, they
warn, to pressure of blood on the brain, and so, at the very first
onset, leap lithely from bed, apply a few leeches, some here,
some there, and then 'chafe the extremities' with a bristly
brush to promote circulation. Then, for good measure, run
rapidly up and down stairs several times. Back in bed (one can
only hope that the sleeping-partner, if any, is also a fellow-
insomniac: he or she will be so by now, in any case), you'll
soon find yourself nodding off, and this particular handy hint
ends with a quotation, for our authors have a literary bent,
about 'Tired Nature's sweet restorer, balmy sleep' which
ought to be by Shakespeare but isn't.

Throughout the book our authorities are quite tremendously bothered about constipation. It is a recurrent theme, a
leitmotif to off-set the pleasant domestic background. Once
again, it is a series of no-nonsense treatments that are
recommended and we find ourselves in a whirl of brimstone
and treacle and munching rhubarb pills and senna pods and
'bruised ginger' and swigging draughts and heaven knows
what else. There is a tendency to suggest all these remedies
even in cases where the recipients are not costive at all — a
sort of method of getting the joyous season of Spring off to a
flying start.

This Victorian preoccupation with aperients, whether
needed or not, spilled over, alas, into my own childhood. At
my prep school, there was every term a dread morning when
Matron, freshly starched and looking purposeful, appeared
with the rising bell clutching a tumbler hideously filled with an
appalling liquid called Gregory Powder. There was no
question at all of not drinking it for she hung over one till the
last explosive drop had gone down. It caused violent griping

pains and necessitated one's almost permanent absence from the classroom. The name of the medicament, I always felt, properly belonged to some business tycoon. 'And now I will ask our chairman, Sir Gregory Powder, to make his report,' which, at a guess, would be a deafening one.

In the book we frequently wander off to other subjects and various valuable tips for healthy, gracious living. For example, always have ready to hand a large piece of baize to throw over any female who may suddenly burst into flames. Don't forget that singing (well, look at the Germans!) is an excellent corrective for pulmonic complaints. On no account open bedroom windows at night. Cure corns by pressing hot potato skins onto them. And then, back we hasten to our old subject and castor oil and cream of tartar, followed by a really electrifying section on enemas. A further short breather in the shape of instructions as to how to prevent pitting after smallpox, how to cure apoplexy (leeches to the temples), how to rid yourself of nervousness (horseback riding, of all things, and at dawn at that), and how to protect dahlias from earwigs, and then it's dear old aperients again and powdered aloes and gamboge and Venice turpentine and the purgative roots of jalap.

Oh and by the way, put paid to flatulence with Angostura Bark, which, I suppose, is what produces angostura bitters and is palatable enough provided that it is extremely closely associated with gin. Quite a lot of gin. If it removes flatulence at the same time, well and good. Perhaps when you visit me on my sick (*sic*) bed, you may care to bring along gin instead of whisky. Or both.

WALKABOUT

I have, at 'Myrtlebank', access to five bedrooms of varying sizes, none of them large, but in point of fact it was the smallest of the lot that I chose for myself. I prefer a bijou bedroom. Snugger. Everything to hand. One has merely to reach out and that freshly laundered pair of cerise y-fronts is there. I suppose that if I went to a professional trick-cyclist for an explanation of this preference, I should eventually pay him £874 and he would finally tell me, nodding sagely, that I have a womb-complex. Well, and why not? It was cosy there all right, as far as one can recall. Another advantage that the room possesses is that one of its windows looks out over both the spacious garden and the orchard, where a pair of odious magpies are currently availing themselves of buckshee pickaback rides on the uncomplaining sheep, and from my bed I can see, beyond the apple trees and the village road, the steeply climbing wooded hill that goes up and away into the horizon and becomes, before very long, Dartmoor. The rising sun hits the hill fair and square and lights up the treetops and there are less agreeable sights to see on waking. As so often, I count my blessings ('483, 484, 485 . . . ').

It is my custom, first thing, to switch on the bedside wireless (Radio Three, natch) which, in addition to its innumerable musical pleasures, both intentional and unintentional (*such* lovely muddles, and very occasionally the wrong record put on at the wrong speed), has a delightfully short news bulletin, a mere five minutes or so of depression. Listening to the eight a.m. news the other day, with half an ear (some blessed physical reaction induces in me a partial deafness when there is any mention of Zimbabwe-Rhodesia, unions, Leyland and something called 'the shopfloor', where everybody seems to be almost permanently ratty), I suddenly heard the words 'tangerine oranges' and 'eucalyptus'. Though instantly put on the alert by even a mention of such unusual and welcome news items (eucalyptus is, as you'll know, a member of the myrtle family and therefore of especial interest here), I missed the full drift and had, all excitement and attention, to wait eagerly until the repeat at nine a.m. I then found that it is hoped that, when all the oil and petrol have been idiotically wasted and squandered and have finally run out, a propulsive power in liquid form can be obtained from both these jewels in the crown of the vegetable world.

In the case of tangerine oranges, I fancy they must mean tangerines in their natural and fresh-off-the-tree, more or less, Christmassy state rather than those attractive little segments that come in tins and find their way eventually into small glass 'sweet' bowls where they breathe their last, smothered beneath a foamy cloud of synthetic cream. As with eucalyptus, it must be some substance that is squeezed from the bark of the tree, or collected in a cup, like gum, or pressed from the skins, or distilled from the stalks. Or something. Anyhow, hooray for it. As the only other alternative propulsive power that I know of, and which isn't going to run out, is the fumes from chicken dung, oranges are a pleasant variant. A crate of tangerines on the car roof is aesthetically more pleasing and in other ways, not the least of which is hygiene, greatly preferable to a coop of clucking Wyandottes forgetting themselves.

However, and although I myself shall never like to see Four-Star Tangerine being dispensed at the pumps, any propulsive power that removes the necessity to walk is quite all right with me. One of the great hazards of spending country weekends with kind friends is the dread Sunday morning phrase: 'Care for a stroll?' (Any host who issued the invitation on a Sunday afternoon would automatically be condemning the quality and calorie-content of the lunch, together with the volume of wine. Sunday afternoons are one of the very few of God's sensible creations and are for snoozing in.) Max Beerbohm, a wise authority on many subjects, his thoughts expressed in a prose so perfect that it is an audacity even to mention him on this page, was not at all in favour of walking in company ('My objection to it is that it stops the brain'). Sir Max considered that the liveliest minds become leaden, the most sparkling eyes become dimmed as the bodies containing them trudge along, grimly reading out whatever notices they chance to see ('Uxminster. Eleven miles'). At boarding schools it was considered essential, and for both sexes, to take a bracing hour and a half walk on a Sunday. Inactivity was perilous. Heaven knows what unscheduled activities might not follow.

And now, bless me, here comes a book called quite simply *Walk!*, rather a peremptory, not to say impertinent, title I would have thought. The sub-title is 'It Could Change Your Life' (in my case by removing it). Never mind. Its author, John Man, looks immensely jolly and the numerous illustrations show him walking like mad in all directions, the very picture of bouncing health. Although the well-named Mr Man lives with his family in the Oxford area, he is, I fancy, American (the word 'humour', of which there isn't really all that much, comes out as 'humor') and, anxious for us to share his enthusiasms, details the pleasures of walking in what one would have thought of as being the least profitable of places. There is a happy snap of beefy Mr Man striding out down New York City's Sixth Avenue and 'sensing the human pulse of a supposedly impersonal city'. This novelty is followed by a vibrant *pensée* from somebody called Donald Culross Peattie (why can so few Americans settle for just the two names?) in his book *The Joy of Walking*: 'To enjoy City walking to the utmost you have to throw yourself into a mood of loving humanity.' Yes indeed. The next time D.C. Peattie is in London, let him test out his love of humanity among passengers attempting to buy tickets for the Northern Line during the rush-hour at Tottenham Court Road Underground Station.

Further *pensées* dot the text and before long we come upon one of those alarming 'tables', devised in this case and with the best intentions by the Michigan Heart Association and which are intended to be a rough guide (using age, weight, habits) to help you to determine whether or not your current life style is going to bring you, sooner or later, to a sudden seizure. The table is headed 'Are You At Risk?'. Well, er, sort of. Nor is one's peace of mind increased by what follows — another table called 'The Rahe Stress Index'. Life's possible misfortunes and stresses are listed, with their seriousness allotted score marks in brackets, maximum one hundred. For example, and from a list that ranges widely, we find Change in Residence (twenty), Jail Term (sixty-three), Death of Spouse (one hundred), Foreclosure of Mortgage (thirty-one), Trouble with the Boss (twenty-three) and Christmas (twelve). The total stress should not ideally come to more than one hundred a week and, as you see, if at Christmas time your spouse has passed across while you are in jail, which itself involves a Change in Residence, you're in a bit of a pickle.

I am not myself really tremendously keen on helpful Mr Man's suggestion for finding out whether one is plump or not ('Assessing Your Fat Content' is, I fear, the title of this section). It is called the 'inch-of-pinch test'. 'Find a book an inch thick,' he says (I hovered between *The Card* and *Precious Bane*, finally settling for *The Daisy Chain*), 'then take the flesh at the side of your waist between your thumb and index finger. If the fold is more than an inch thick . . .' Need I say more? 'Each inch is estimated to equal forty pounds of fat.' Another method of testing, though hardly more acceptable, is to use 'skin-fold calipers' with two pincers or arms that 'lock onto the fold of skin in such a way that you can record the size of the gap in between the two pincers'. Then hasten to your table showing the 'Skin-fold Conversion Factors' and learn the worst.

74

Not even a flowery *pensée* which goes ' The magic of the moccasin still makes good medicine' is going to change my non-walking habits. But if I am ever by mistake coaxed out against my will (the Bultitudes are for ever shrieking 'Join us for a tramp' over the hedge), I have thought of a splendid method of revenge. Reverting, and without difficulty, to childhood, I shall, after 400 yards, sit down by the side of the road and say: 'I'm tired. Carry me.'

TRUMPET VIGOROUSLY

Musing away here in the bosky garden of 'Myrtlebank' (May trees and laburnums in full glory, their colours skilfully non-clash: climbing roses just starting to burst), my thoughts sometimes wander back down memory's increasingly confused lanes to an area that is still sharp and clear in the mind, my prep school on the Hampshire coast. Sharp and clear in the nostrils too are the peculiar smells of the corridors' brown linoleum, the stoke-hole off the bathroom, the boot-room, and Matron's 'den'. It wasn't really a topnotch prep school, I'm afraid. I don't much go in for sour strictures of the past and I merely have a sense of wonderment that the school's many and strange imperfections should have been allowed to be. From lunch (one p.m.) on, there was nothing whatever to eat but bread scraped with margarine, the dry and sulky hunks revealing the irritation of the skivvies, as we called them, who had unlovingly prepared this digestible treat. To make the hunks more interesting, we spread them with mustard. At evening prayers, a cup of some weak beef extract appeared, swiftly swallowed and usually in a state of great trepidation as prayer time was, unsuitably enough when all should have been forgiveness and amity, the moment chosen by the headmaster, at that moment of the day awash with whisky and peevishness, for picking on various victims and twisting their ears. At bedtime the hungrier boys ate their toothpaste. Nobody ran away. We hadn't the strength.

We were all issued (sixpence on the bill) with an improving little booklet called *Self Helps to Self and Fitness* which aimed at producing both the mind serene and the body beautiful. After a foreword on the importance of regular habits, the opening sentence of the main body of the work ran: 'On waking, trumpet vigorously to clear nostrils.' 'To trumpet', we learnt, meant to snort noisily outwards. The author was a master at the school, a wonky giant who taught French extremely well and added to this ability various unscheduled extras when opportunity presented itself. He himself led the way by trumpeting vigorously throughout the day, a sadly catarrhal figure. When in the open, he chose to trumpet and snuffle without benefit of handkerchief, finger and thumb to nose. I have seen others do this since and as a spectacle I haven't ever come to love it. With the aid of the *Self Helps*, we ran here, doubled there, threw this and held that, our minds sullenly unreceptive and by no means serene. We benefited, I don't doubt, bodily but I've never enjoyed being coerced into any violent physical movement, apart from those that come quite naturally such as running for a bus or nimbly dodging cars or playing Scrabble, and since leaving the school (it was 1924) and abandoning *Self Helps*, I've rather let that side of things slide.

But now, troubled again, I have been handed *Total Fitness*, a glowingly recommended paperback and of dual authorship, Lawrence E. Morehouse and Leonard Gross, who, in a preface, give grateful thanks to those human guinea-pigs who 'voluntarily exercised to exhaustion' in laboratories to establish the cheering news that a desirable level of 'fitness' can be yours without strain and sweat. The authors are, of course, American and make much use of the phrase 'to get in shape'. Well, I certainly have, like anybody else, a shape. So far, so good. And there is further comfort to be found. 'The best position for the shoulders is hanging loose to the sides.' Why, that's just exactly where mine are.

Though I am, I discover, an 'endomorph' (the dictionary gives 'a person of rounded build'), I prefer to ignore our authors when they talk about 'bouncing flab' and to concentrate on the less insulting and more thoughtful side of their deliberations. Callisthenics aimed at cultivating gracefulness and strength originated, we find, in Sweden in the last century, rich Swedish landowners finding the sight of their stooped and sagging peasants so offensive that they instigated physical drill (hence, I suppose, Swedish drill) to improve posture at the plough and in the barn (the stoopers and saggers were absurdly grateful, no doubt). And goodness me the physical myths that Messrs Morehouse and Gross encouragingly explode on all sides: there is no reason at all for abstinence and keeping off you-know-what before a competitive athletics fixture (indeed, you may perhaps fly even faster down the track), or for not eating before swimming (at the 1968 Olympics a young swimmer ate a sizeable hamburger with onions, four candy bars and drank a Coke and then broke her own world record, triumphing both over her rivals and her hiccoughs).

Once again I look the other way when our authors hammer on with their anti-obesity message ('you can see the fat hanging from your body in pendulous folds') and rejoin them when they are in sunnier mood and providing useful charts which demonstrate how many calories there are per food portion and what duration of exercise is necessary to get rid of them. Thus, to remove the effects of one fried egg and a baked potato, I have to ski (downhill, thank God) for twenty minutes. For one pancake, it's a run (!) of seven minutes. If I lose my head completely and wolf down a plate of 'cereal', two tablespoons of sugar, some tinned tuna, and a rissole with French fried on the side, I must either play tennis for two hours or garden for three or do 'bowling' (surely not energetic enough?) for four. But here, as with so much in the book, there is a relatively easy way out. I note that eighty minutes of 'reclining in bed' removes one hundred calories, and so, for the smallish snack mentioned above, I just slip between the sheets for five hours and I'm as good as new.

There's just so much else. Why not try the Fitness Hop to

the rhythm off *Tea for Two*? There's the 'Ask Yourself Who You Are!' section, a challenge to anybody. There's advice on the modish custom of 'jogging', which must in my case be on-the-spot jogging rather than at a slow lope through our village, where it would spread alarm and despondency. All through the day as we go about our normal round, we can be exercising. If there's a typewriter to be moved, 'welcome the opportunity'. Stand up, they advise, when you take all telephone calls. Spring about in general. At a conference, jump to your feet to make a point and 'pace about'. We're trying, you see, to restore and build up the muscles of our abdominal walls rather than build up our popularity. On returning home, 'treat yourself to some extravagant motions', such as 'yanking open all the kitchen cabinets'. Feverishly, while the calories fly off, 'polish a pan' or rearrange your library. Do all this and, it seems, with reasonable luck you will live longer, though I am in some doubt whether in these circumstances, this is a sensible target to aim at.

RUBENS WAS RIGHT

I bring cheerful news for those of us who, firmly resisting less pleasant descriptions of our bodily condition (Americans, not the most sensitive people in the world, make much use of that distasteful word 'flab' and tend to refer to us collectively as 'chubbos'), like to regard ourselves rather as being attractive pink plumpnesses, providers of firm healthy flesh, and plenty of it, for all to admire.

A close study of both literature and art leads me to the agreeable conclusion that it is in every way jollier and more acceptable to be, in a wine connoisseur's term, 'pleasantly rounded' and that success in life and social popularity and a generous embonpoint have often gone, all three of them, hand in hand and continue to do so today. Everything points to the fact that fortune favours fatties.

Just consider. Not even the most sycophantic painter could ever depict Napoleon with a tummy that did anything but bulge, and just look at him — an Emperor entirely by his own efforts, a thing which happens to but few. Remember, if you will, the robust, to put it mildly, Prince Regent, a genial and jocular fellow if ever there was one, loved by all and the talk of Brighton. Many playgoers will happily recall Yvonne Arnaud, that gurgling, enchanting roly-poly French actress who increased in vivacious charm as the platform of her scales sank ever lower and her needle wobbled wider. Down the years her pretty little face acquired, as Lilian Braithwaite observed, another little face round it. Well then, who could possibly imagine Nell Gwynne as being even remotely skinny,

80

and she went places that subsequently owed nothing to oranges. Churchill, at the most important period of his life (and, indeed, of ours), was what might politely be called 'chunky', a national saviour more given to saying a firm 'No' to Hitler than to calories.

And in literature what does one find? An authority as distinguished as Sir Walter Scott, from the land of baps and girdle-cakes and porridge and other splendidly fattening foods, spoke up admiringly for the advantages of being 'fair, fat and forty', though some women, forty being such a thought-provoking milestone in the feminine life-span, may prefer to think of themselves as being permanently fair, fat and thirty-nine, and very nice too. Then there was Julius Caesar, a clever man who, apart from an inability to dodge, had almost everything going for him. His opinion must surely still be of value and it was an opinion that came down very heavily (and very rightly and bloodily, as things turned out) against people with lean and hungry looks. 'Such men are dangerous' was his view.

And dangerous, goodness knows, they still are in the shape of the would-be lean and probably hungry joggers who everywhere now come out at dusk like bats, go blundering along the country's pavements and knock pedestrians into the gutter. Never has there been a more ridiculous fad and some soon see the futility of this modish pastime. A friend of mine who lives in central London and likes to be in the swim, took up jogging and was pounding along at eventide in the W1 area when suddenly he caught sight of himself reflected in a Bond Street shop window and was so unnerved by the appalling and outlandish spectacle that he took a taxi home and straightway hung up his shorts. And let us never forget the fine example of Lady Antonia Fraser who announced that she abandoned jogging on the shaming day when she found her children *walking* past her.

A recent visit to the National Gallery strongly supports my contention that a proper respect and admiration for obesity exists and is rapidly gaining ground. How many art lovers will you find in front of El Greco's etiolated and gangling figures, painful to view in their boniness and not one of whom has, obviously, munched a doughnut in years? Very few, and some of them are only there because they are on their way, expectantly polishing their glasses, to somewhere else, namely the lusher pastures, the wonderfully opulent forms and faces and the altogether more voluptuous human material provided by the painter Rubens.

I used the words 'the altogether' advisedly in order to ring a bell in memory's chambers and to warn those hitherto unaware of the art of Rubens that it is in the altogether that he is so supreme. Vast and rosy expanses of flesh are to be seen on all sides, with everybody looking as jolly and happy as can be. Scarcely a shoulder is draped. Not a single skinny lizzie is visible. Backs are fully exposed to view, ditto waists, although very few of Rubens' ladies and gentlemen have actually bothered about retaining their waists. Rich and overlapping folds of pink human tissue do very well instead.

Not all of Rubens' masterpieces are, of course, in our possession and present in this country but reproductions of his other pictures are freely available and tell the same heartening story. In a very famous one called *The Toilet of Venus*, the lady is seen from, as it were, behind and there is really rather a lot of her and it on view (the dusky handmaiden attending her and who is to be seen at the ready with combs and kirbygrips and the lacquer hair spray is plainly proud indeed to be serving such a bold expanse of mistress). A trip to one of Europe's museums and hey presto, you could be feasting your eyes on *The Sleeping Angelica*, a lady who has been merrily notching up the carbohydrates (the word 'jumbo' springs instantly to mind) and, wandering through the woods, had decided to strip off, rest awhile and snatch forty winks. And while in the Land of Nod she has been 'surprised' by a hermit who appears to be very far from displeased by this wholehearted display of avoirdupois.

At the drop of a hat, or of almost anything at all, Rubens' figures throw discretion and their clothes to the winds, and presumably his models did the same. As a result one wouldn't give tuppence for poor Mrs Rubens' peace of mind as, visualising an abundance of bare arms and legs, she kisses her husband goodbye ('Have a nice day, dear') before he sets off, a fresh tube of carmine at the ready, for a gruelling morning in his Antwerp *atelier*. How fortunate for him that the Dutch, by nature neither a shy nor slim race, matched his mood.

Not that our gifted artist ever oversteps the bounds of propriety. Rubens is skilful indeed with little wisps of gauze. His ladies tend to bring along with them little gauze scarves, and from the scarves little wisps hang down here and there and do a fine concealment job. There are even little wisps present in the picture of Hercules, a fine figure of a man if ever there was one, though here the little wisps' masking requirement is a rather more extensive one. All is, however, safely gathered in and the prudish can breathe again.

On the National Gallery visit of which I spoke, I came upon a sizeable group of admirers gazing eagerly at one particular Rubens painting and, peering round heads and over shoulders, I saw that it was *The Rape of the Sabines*. What a very animated and unusual scene! There is a point to notice right away, and a comforting one. The rapacious gentlemen, obviously anxious to be up and away with their dazzlingly beautiful prizes, manage to stifle what must have been a momentary gasp of misgiving at the actual weight of the feminine booty to be loaded onto horseback and carried off. Instead they wear nothing but pleased expressions. 'This is a fun assignment,' they are clearly thinking. The ladies too, though for the moment agitated at the prospect of such a sudden and unexpected journey ('My dear, we didn't have time to pack a *thing*!'), are plainly far from displeased by the sturdy torsos and prominent calf muscles and bulging biceps of their abductors. Gazing at this fine picture, the first anxious concern of those of us who possess any sort of social instinct must be to wonder whether there are going to be quite enough Sabine women to, so to speak, go round. However, feverishly totting them up, male and female and not overlooking that distant band of horsemen galloping up to join in the fun, the sexes seem to be just about evenly balanced, give or take a virgin or two.

And now, having as good as proved that it pays to be plump, how are we going to set about achieving the pleasantly padded physical state that ensures smiles all round and makes us new friends by the dozen? It is only in the twentieth century, a misguided and idiotic assembly of years if ever I saw one, and dangerous and disastrous to boot, that our country has gone in, and in a really serious way, for banting. Like silly sheep, we follow on where others lead, piously declining animal fats and anything farinaceous. You would never catch prominent European races, though foolish enough in many other ways, regretfully shaking their heads when the potatoes are coming round. No Swiss, inventors of so much that is finest and best in the sweetmeat world, is truly happy without having his fingers in a box of chocs and feeling for a violet centre. Try to imagine a happy Italian couple refusing yet another heaped mound of pasta, or a Frog family without at least three of those vast and crusty loaves, so delicious with butter.

Off we go then with a sensible breakfast. 'You're the cream in my coffee' ran a line in an adulatory and popular song of the 1920s, and a very good way to start the day too. Out of the window fly those artificial sweeteners (and the disquieting medical rumours connected with them) and into the coffee cup go popping three lumps of sugar. Oh all right then, four. 'Is there anything in the world nicer than a lightly boiled egg?' people sometimes wistfully ask, not expecting an answer though an answer is ready and waiting. Yes, there is. Two lightly boiled eggs. And we are not forgetting a rack of freshly made toast, with brioches nestling and keeping warm in a napkin, and a selection of what hotels will call 'preserves' (black cherry jam a must), and the butter moulded into those lovely little nobbly balls, and a jug of fresh orange juice (I hope you've already had a refreshing glass of it before attacking the porridge with which, more cream, breakfast began). And there you are, all set up for the day and with a mere two hours to go before the little feast that merry ladies, just back from shopping in Guildford ('I got held up in Sainsbury's'), refer to as 'elevenses', a British snackette closely connected with home-made cake.

There is one item that appears frequently on almost all diet sheets as being, in the view of the compilers of these loveless documents, laudably free of anything that is going to delight the body. I refer to peppers, red or green, take your choice. Although, I must admit, attractive to the eye (why not string a few together, in alternate colours, and wear them as a novel necklace at Nigel and Caroline's next little cheese-and-wine 'do'?), they contain, as Grandma Buggins used to grumble in her wartime food broadcasts, 'nothing to clash yer teeth into'. I find them tough and indigestible and totally deficient in nutritional interest, negative virtues which ensure their constant appearance at the tables of those who have not yet seen the light.

Away, then, with peppers and for lunch on with the steak and kidney pudding (so much richer and more succulent than pie), the new potatoes glistening with butter (four makes a nice round number), the cauliflower lusciously lurking beneath its white sauce. Munch up! And don't forget to leave room for that baked jam roll. Chubbos of the World Unite! Pass on the good news. Flab is fab.

DO BRING YOUR GONG ALONG

We may be fairly remote down here in Devon and there are those who picture us as being permanently knee-deep in clotted cream and bemused with heady cider, but in point of fact we keep a sharp eye on things and my friends and I, alert as ever, were greatly astonished to read in the paper that the agricultural, fisheries and food section of Her Majesty's Government, represented by Mr Edward Bishop, with Mrs Bishop loyally at his side, had thrown a gladsome 'reception' at a Nottingham hotel. And on whose behalf do you suppose they trundled all the way up to the Dukeries? Who were there to sip the medium Cyprus and crowd hungrily to the tasty cold buffet? Why, your and my top-favourite group of fun people — none other than the International Institute of Sugar Beet Researchers. How the researchers found time to break off from their arduous beet research duties, down tools in Toulouse, Trieste and the vinegar vats of Tarragona and hook it hastily for that prime beet centre, Nottingham, *qui sait* and *quien sabe*? Can it be that 1977, in addition to the joyous (and I mean it) Jubilee, is to be the year when the mysterious, legend-enshrouded sugar beet, a shy comestible if ever there was one, is at last to yield up its strange secret? If so, hooray indeed. At this sensational gathering (paid for, as I'm always reminding you, by us), were suitable toasts drunk ('Gentlemen, I give you the humble beet')? Were speeches made, urging the researchers on to ever more violent researching?

Sugar beet isn't perhaps, as a springboard for eloquence, the absolutely ideal subject but how odd it is that certain voices

can make even the most arid material pleasing. Sir John
Gielgud could recite, to non-cricket-lovers, page after page
of *Wisden*'s past excitements ('Hammond, run out, 84.
Hobbs, hit wicket, 197') and make them fully pleasurable.
During the war, the frightening edge was taken off the direst of
disasters by, on the radio, the calm and comforting tones of
Stuart Hibberd. But odder still is the fact that these two
sterling performers, both famous too for their modesty,
would, like most of the rest of us, shrink with horror and
dismay at the sound of their own recorded voices. We don't,
the informed tell me, hear our own voices through our own
ears. Though it seems probable that a whisper or two comes
floating round the corner, so to speak, the main volume of
sound makes its way, it seems, by a more direct route and
along some solid bone conductor inside one's nut and reaches
the ear-drums that way. We do not, fortunately, flinch all the
time as we speak, for we are clearly hearing something
different and, to us, tolerable. It is only on listening to our
recorded voices that we get the true and horrible vocal impact.
Some people cannot accept it. Edith Evans, recorded by the
BBC in the '20s, refused to believe that those wild swoops
and whoops and ululations and flutings were from her own
unusual organ. ('Take it off,' she shrieked, 'there's been a
muddle.') It was Dame Edith too who, starring in a play and
finding that Kenneth Williams was to join her in the cast,
raised an initial objection ('But he's got such a peculiar
voice!')

I was first forced to listen to my own affected and
pretentious and namby-pamby tones in the mid-'30s. I had
started to make gramophone records for Columbia. The
records were intended to be funny and, as in those days
Columbia's recording artistes, as we were tastefully called,
had each to be inserted into a conveniently descriptive slot for
the catalogue, my little wax offerings were issued to the public
labelled *Humorous Monologues*, both to me extremely off-
putting words. I had to 'pass' each record (I made one a

year) and therefore had to listen, horrified, to them as they came out. I have never risked the experience since.

But being, in the '30s, youngish and keen and anxious to improve, I buried my nose in various books on elocution and found myself at once in a fascinating world of physical technicalities. The writers were for ever encouraging me to open my mouth and, peering inside it with the aid of a glass, to feast my eyes on my hard and soft palates, my tongue, my glottis, my laryngeal areas, and, somewhere at the back, my 'little grape-shaped pendant', or uvula. Moving a bit further afield and in a southerly direction, there was my larynx going excitingly up and down, and my Adam's apple which, nowadays snugly enfolded, has not been on view since about 1948. Great stress seemed to be laid on the desirability of a musical laugh and the texts were thick with 'Ha! Ha! Ha!' on a rising or descending scale, or a hearty 'Ho! Ho! Ho!' right there on the very same note. Speaking was referred to as 'phonation' and the pages bristled with lively vocal exercises ('Hurrah! Hurry! Harry! Harriet!').

I have recently dealt, in an egocentric manner, both with my phobias and my physique and now, in what I promise to be a final attempt at improving my image, I'm into elocution again, greatly helped by Malcolm Morrison's handy little *Clear Speech* whose worthy aim is to get us all articulating crisply enough to avoid 'a time-wasting flurry of pardon me's'. We are also invited to emulate, in stunning clarity, various speakers and among them a BR station announcer called Angela Peberdy who must, alas, announce at a station that I have not yet had the pleasure of visiting (there used to be a lovely lady at Taunton who welcomed the train's arrival with a glad cry of 'Torn-tun, Torn-tun'). In addition to the Voice Beautiful, Mr Morrison is insistent on the vital importance of Posture. Before so much as a single syllable is uttered, get that Posture right. It's far from easy. Follow closely. Don't slump. Don't push the torso forwards and upwards. 'The pelvis should be directly above the instep. The torso should be directly above the pelvis. The shoulders should be directly above the pelvis and in line with the breast bone at the front.' There is also advice on double chins (avoidance of) which comes a bit late in the day for some.

But it is in the choice of piquant phrases for exercising the vocal cords that Mr Morrison's true forte lies (indeed, it is to him that we owe 'Bring your gong along'). At first, of course, we have to work through valuable but meaningless sounds such as OOTHOO, AWSTHS and HAW HAW HAW (I thought it wouldn't be long before we got to laughter). But soon after that a jolly note is struck with 'many merry milkmaids' and 'nineteen noisy gnomes', and what could be more dramatic than 'The snake stung swiftly', 'The blood flowed slowly' and 'The flames leapt into the loft'? Occasionally there is a puzzlement. What can 'filthy gold silk' be, and why is it filthy? There are, too, a few improbabilities: 'Wendy watched the weasel walking' and 'You lose too many shoes!' 'Take a tube to Tewkesbury' is merely misleading and might get foreigners into serious difficulties at Piccadilly Underground ('We are requiring two days returns to Tewkesbury'). And then suddenly all is jollity again with 'Twenty tiny tap dancers' and 'Two dukes tooting tunes on little flutes'. Nor are politics neglected. 'The assassination of the assistant secretary surprised several people', as well it might. But here too is a political puzzlement. 'Harold fell and yelled for help.' Well, I suppose that, in a sense, he certainly fell, but I've heard no yells for help, yet.

UNDER PRESSURE

Apart from the somewhat outlandish and improbable names that one sometimes has to memorise and get one's tongue round (Darlene Porter Mandelbaum; Byron C. Scharnhorst the Third), nobody raises a louder hurrah than I for the entire American race with their warm-heartedness and generosity and, gasp with surprise as some readers may, what one can only call their goodness, a goodness of which most other countries, cynically disbelieving in the possibility anywhere of such a national characteristic, have a dark and instinctive suspicion. My enthusiasm for the American language is more guarded. It is true that it occasionally enriches English with marvellously succinct little phrases ('I want out' is a crisp example) but at the same time it falls rather too often unpleasingly on the ear. I've never somehow got accustomed to the two words 'heavy petting'. The activities they describe are neither here nor there. It's just the words that I'm unkeen on. They occur in those deadly serious articles about virginity statistics among sophomores at, say, universities in the mid-West and when I say deadly I mean deadly. The poor old adjective 'heavy' never seems anyway to hook itself on to anything very joyous — heavy-hearted, heavy weather, heavy-handed, heavy breathing.

Where can one lay the blame for the currently all too fashionable word 'pressures'? Hardly on America, I think, but much nearer home. The word comes in handy in courtrooms when two merry, curly-headed teenagers, apprehended by the police after battering and chopping to bits an ancient grandmother and robbing her of seventy pence, are being politely invited to explain their nowadays not very unusual conduct. The defence psychiatrist duly trots out his balmy speech (balmy in the sense of course of providing balm) about the boys' action being but a simple 'cry for help'. The pressures referred to are, presumably, the worrying prospect of having, some day and in some fashion (and if not, there's always Assistance) to earn a living, coupled with society's strange insistence that they should stop bashing people about. As pressures go, these hardly seem to amount to very much. Cockney slum-dwellers of the 1890s might have had a justifiable thought or two about pressures. It is odd that forty years ago in the, for so many, threadbare '30s and earlier in the deplorable '20s when there was every reason to complain, nobody whined about pressures and old grannies could sleep peacefully in their beds. Remarkable that at a time when severe poverty and need were a permanent feature of life, honesty and reasonable behaviour flourished too. Perhaps some psychiatrist could examine these puzzling facts and come up with another balmy (as before) explanation.

So much for pressures but we can, I think, allow another modish word, that of 'tension' and all that it implies. Tension seems to me entirely understandable in a world which includes President Amin, cod, Russia, jukeboxes, Mr Healey's financial pronouncements, the Metropolitan (or any other of your choice) Waterboard, oil, and those charming new nerve bombs which are said to pick people, seated at breakfast and deep in the crossword, neatly off while leaving completely unscathed the impressive facade of fourteen Chatsworth Crescent, Bognor.

However, let us all cheer up for I bring, as so often, comfort and help in the shape of *Simple Relaxation*, delightful Laura Mitchell's physiological method of easing tension. If you imagine that you are already *au fait* with and 'into' relaxation and that it just means going ker-flop on your new duvet and passing smoothly out, then I have news for you. Relaxation is a problem you've got actually to work hard at and Miss Mitchell's informative pages are crammed with illustrations of her happy patients pulling this limb and lengthening that and twiddling joints in all directions, success everywhere. To show the other side of the medal, however, there is included an apparently happy snap of 'Mrs Denis Healey being interviewed in 1974' which reveals her, we discover, doing quite everything she shouldn't and proving to be a prime tension victim, displaying every known symptom ('head pushed forward, neck practically vanished, spine curved, elbows bent, hands clenched and legs crossed'). She has, alas, since 1974 had cause to curve her spine and clench her hands and lose her neck altogether.

We start strongly with Chapter One ('Disease spells Dis-Ease') and press thrillingly on with Nerves, Muscles and Fear (a biblical quotation always creates confidence and here our authoress has selected 'I am fearfully and wonderfully made,' Psalm 139, v. 14, and all too true). How extraordinary to discover after all this time that one possesses Spindles and Golgi, both names of sensory nerve endings, though I'm far from sure where their province lies or what they get up to down there in the dark. 'Assuming mine is a body under stress,' challenges Miss Mitchell, 'what orders will I give it to change the pattern of stress to a pattern of ease?' The answer that springs immediately to mind is 'Sit right down, dear, and help yourself to an amber-coloured glass of whisky', but I fear that this is frivolous and totally unacceptable. We're here to work and away we go, pulling our shoulders towards our feet, turning our hips outwards, dragging our jaws downwards, stretching limbs right and left while yawning, and lastly, 'pushing our feet away from our face.' As regards this final trick, Miss Mitchell counsels 'Do this rather slowly.' I'm not going to do it *at all*, Miss Mitchell, until I understand exactly what is involved.

It's plain that it all works a treat and tension vanishes if you keep at it, but it is when we come to insomnia that clever Miss

92

Mitchell moves right into top gear. Her view about sleepless-ness is don't just lie there, get up and fight it. We must, once again, be a hive of activity. Before so much as thinking of bed, take Rover for an evening stroll or, possibly, run round the garden a few times. Then bed? Not at all. 'Pamper your tummy' is the order, and pamper it by popping into it some milky beverage or, if you prefer, just slosh in the whisky. Once finally between the sheets, banish tension by running through your joint-easing exercises a time or two before passing on to some activity such as religious meditation or poetry reciting or planning the next week's menus. If wakeful in the night, leap from bed, hasten to the lavatory and none of that shall I or shan't I, and then nip to the kitchen and collect up 'just a little something' (a banana, a handful of Garibaldis), returning to bed with your dorm feed and munching it slowly while reading 'an undemanding book' (there are several about). The tuck, you see, will divert blood to your stomach from your head and leave less to think with. 'Soothe yourself by all these tricks and then swamp your brain with boredom.' No problem.

DEVONSHIRE
CREAM

GOD'S WONDERFUL RAILWAY

'Yes. I thought you looked a Paddington type.'

I have had some strange things said to me in my time and that was among the strangest, uttered quite recently by a cheerful taxi-driver who had picked me up outside my club in Pall Mall and whom I had asked to take me to Paddington, 'Gateway to the West', though I left that addition unsaid.

What on earth, I wondered, could have given me away as an old Great Western addict? It could hardly be my clothing — tweed cap, macintosh, sober slacks and shoes — or my luggage (small suitcase). Fearful of hearing something damaging to my pride, I did not dare to ask what had betrayed me, even though there was, as is now customary, a free exchange of news and views — the state of the pound, Mrs Thatcher's policies, the National Gallery extension — shouted through the pulled-back glass panel. Gone for ever in taxis is the closed window, the silent back of the head, the absence of conversation. A flow of cheery talk is now expected: and very friendly too.

I think that perhaps what the driver meant by 'Paddington type' was simply that I looked happy. I have spent much of my life either boarding trains at Paddington or alighting from them and I have noticed, down the years, a pleased expression on the faces of most of my fellow travellers. After all, they have probably just come from, or are just going to, some of the country's most beautiful places and buildings — the Cornish coastline, the City of Bath, the Welsh mountains, the

97

cathedral at Wells, the Cotswolds, the Exe valley, the rolling Somerset hills.

I have also had occasion in my life to use most of the other main railway stations of London and they make an interesting and varied study. Waterloo produces the harassed look of the bothered business man. Liverpool Street, for some so far away and difficult to get to, is thronged with panting people gasping out: 'I didn't think I was going to make it.' Victoria used to be full of weak stomachs wondering whether the Channel would be choppy. Euston now possesses too few places where you can sit comfortably down and exhaustion is a poor preparation for a lengthy trip north. King's Cross has its points but its trains run to a number of places that hardly rank as beauty spots. But Paddington has it over them all.

I well remember, as a London child, our regular holiday journeys to Ilfracombe and to my grandparents in North Devon. There was in those spacious days a 'through carriage' from Paddington and to save trouble our heavy trunks had already been despatched by Luggage in Advance and would, unbelievably now, precede us without extra charge and would be waiting for us at the other end. We set off about midday and my father used to get a Paddington Railway official to telephone ahead and get them to prepare a luncheon basket for four. This was usually put on for us at Reading (it was a great excitement to see a station restaurant man holding a laden basket aloft and calling our name), though occasionally we had to wait till Newbury (stops were frequent) and once, in mounting suspense and alarm, we waited until the aptly named Hungerford. The basket contained cold chicken joints, bread rolls, butter, buns, cheese and fruit. For my parents there was a half bottle of Hock, my brother and I making do with oranges. The basic cost was, I think, about three shillings a head and the empty basket could be handed out and got rid of at Taunton. Less elaborate refreshment was obtainable from those wheeled and attractively stocked trolleys that paraded the platforms at every stop. They did a fine trade, but now seem, alas, to have vanished.

Shortly after Taunton the train branched off, making amid charming country for Barnstaple and passing through Dulverton and South Molton and, to a child, a funny-sounding station called Morebath (Lessbath was what one was after). And at Barnstaple, full of the smell of the sea, our carriage was uncoupled and soon we set out alone, tugged by a small tank (I suppose) engine, for the steep climb up Devonian tors to Braunton and Morthoe (first actual sight of the sea). The straining puffs of the engine seemed, as we went higher, to be saying 'I-*think*-I-can, I-*think*-I-can, I-*think*-I-can', followed, as we coasted down the slopes into Ilfracombe, by a triumphant 'Thought-I-could, thought-I-could, thought-I-could'. The buffers at Ilfracombe station always looked to me to be insubstantial and flimsy and I feared that we would go crashing through them and down into the town, much of which lay below. But no such calamity occurred.

Everything about trains fascinated me from early on and a little later in life I used to stay with friends in a handsome house in Oxfordshire that had for me the great advantage of being within sight and sound of the railway line that ran, and still blessedly runs, between Oxford and Cheltenham and Worcester. By day there was the exciting view of the beloved chocolate and cream coaches flashing past at an incredible sixty mph (Phew!) but best of all was the night time when, safely tucked up in bed, one could just see the lights of a train (too late to be the Cheltenham Flyer) and hear the occasional whistle. The swoosh of a train as it goes flying through the night is a romantic sound.

Even now and old as I am, I would happily live practically *on* a railway line. I frequently travel nowadays from Paddington to Exeter and as the train winds down the banked curves (there is a speed limit) that lead to the station at Bruton in Somerset, there is on the right a very small house that cannot be more than ten feet from the track. It has a well placed window from which all passing traffic must be visible. I wonder if it is ever for sale.

When in 1921 we left London and went to live in Newbury, it was a comfort to know that our line would be the Great Western. I was sometimes sent on my bicycle to do morning shopping in the town and I used always to time my errands to coincide with the arrival of the Cornish Riviera express, that grandest of all trains, that went whizzing through Newbury non-stop to Plymouth, scooping up water from those troughs near Aldermaston and Frome. It left Paddington at ten-thirty a.m. and ran the whole year round. I think the locomotives in those days were King Class and the journey took four hours. Were there slip-coaches? I dare say so, and the whole gleaming splendour was fully visible from a convenient bridge from which I goggled, entranced.

Many years later I was privileged to have an even closer look at this train of trains. This was when we came to live in Devon in the beautiful Teign Valley and our railway was the pleasant little single track that wound its hilly way between Exeter and Newton Abbot (four trains a day each way). On one occasion when the main line along the coast at Dawlish had been blocked by a landslide, all trains had to be diverted and many made use of our line. On hearing that the Cornish Riviera express was also coming our way, many of us hurried down to the station to give it a welcome and to cheer it on its way. Soon it came majestically into view, carefully rounding our tight curves at a sober fifteen mph or so and picking its way like some elderly dowager caught unexpectedly in a field full of cowpats. Indeed, I shall never forget the haughty looks and upturned noses of the first class passengers, resentful of the diversion and wondering where on earth they had got to. They clearly thought that we were some Peasants' Rising and we would shortly set about them with pitchforks. Our dear little line exists no more but at least its station is still there, transformed into a commodious pink dwelling. I wonder if ghost trains (and who can ever forget the marvellous stage effects in that famous play?) fly past in the silent watches of the night.

Sometimes in our London days we went, instead of to North Devon, to the South and the Dartmoor district (my parents were both keen walkers) and on these occasions one of the many excitements was that we positively travelled on the Cornish Riviera and had lunch (four courses, magically prepared in that tiny kitchen) in the restaurant car. When we arrived at Plymouth's North Road station, we got out and changed platforms for the stopping train up to Yelverton and our Furnished Rooms, a type of holiday accomodation then much more plentiful than hotels. And at Yelverton there was the GWR branch line to Dartmoor and Princetown (an incredible 1,373 feet above sea level) and a gateway to the moor with its wonderful walks and chances of tor-climbing. This remarkable line, built in 1883, was an engineering triumph with its innumerable curves winding ever upwards (my father always insisted, as a joke for juveniles, that if you were to lean out of the end coach you would be able to shake hands with the engine driver, so sharp were the bends). The names of the stations, if such they may be called (a single wooden platform six feet wide), are with me to this day — Burrator Halt, King Tor Halt, Ingra Tor Halt. We used them all, either as a starting place for a walk or to bear us away, exhausted, at the end of the day.

Maps of the South and West of England stir endless railway memories. A troop train after the Dunkirk evacuation that found its way onto the GWR network and tipped us all out at an army camp near Castle Cary. A childhood journey with my Cousin Madge along the spectacular Welsh coast to Tenby when we sat in first class seats with third class tickets, risking, or so I feared, instant imprisonment. Once at Didcot I remember an agitated old gentleman rushing up and down shouting: 'But I *must* have a seat in a lavatory compartment' (they very hastily made room for him).

And then, on 8 January, 1985, my great enthusiasm for

101

railways and my love, for such it is, of the ghost of the GWR
reached their peak when I was invited to sit in the driving cab
of a High Speed Train and make the thrilling trip from Bristol
to Plymouth. It is, I suppose, fitting that this, one of
childhood's prime ambitions, should have been achieved in
my second (almost) childhood. Not, I hasten to reassure
anxious passengers, that I was allowed actually to drive the
train but, perched up beside the driver, within reach of the
controls and with the breath-taking view ahead along the
shining rails, I could imagine that I was in charge.

Oddly enough there was no impression of real speed. The
dial said that we were doing ninety mph but it seemed like
forty: and when we slowed to forty we seemed to be barely
moving. Built-in safety devices caused bells and buzzers to
sound from time to time, their purpose explained to me by the
genial drivers. Occasionally warning notices indicated track
repairs (cheerful waves were exchanged with the workers) and
sometimes a distant signal forbade fast onward progress. As
instructed by trackside notices saying either W (WHISTLE)
or SW (SOUND WHISTLE, I assume), we dutifully
whistled, or rather we made that distinctive High Speed two-
note honking noise (what else to call it?) that carries for miles.
If the road ahead was level or downhill and we had reached
ninety, the limit for the run, the driver shut off power and we
coasted along under our own momentum and for an appre-
ciable time without dropping speed. We could run thus for
many miles and I was told of a train that, making for
Paddington, ran out of fuel ten miles out and managed to get
into the station, all the signals being friendly, without
difficulty.

Perhaps the best part of the trip was when we left Exeter and
ran along the side of the Exe estuary and, reaching the coast at
Dawlish Warren, negotiated the sea-wall with its many
curves, bends, tunnels and rocky outcrops: and so into
Teignmouth and up along the Teign estuary and its birds,
boats and muddy smells. Then on to Newton Abbot and

Totnes and up to the heights of Rattery and South Brent, and thence the long downhill glide into Plymouth. Frequently the journey became like something in an agreeable dream and I had to keep pinching myself. Enjoyment was total and I could have sat there for ever.

MY COUNTY, MY COUNTY

In the days before canned music and the wireless and telly existed, amateur bass and baritone singers, rumbling away at the Bechstein in Victorian drawing-rooms like so many Peter Dawsons, did a noisy good service to England's finest county. 'In Devon,' they boomed, 'in Devon, Glorious Devon,' thus doing something to counter the damaging rumour, obviously spread by envious Cornishmen, that when the Pilgrim Fathers sailed away from Plymouth they were not so much anxious to get to America as to get away from Devon at all costs. The two counties do not love each other. Strange that the invisible boundary line that keeps them apart should be as arboreally visible as that between Spain and Portugal. On the one side there is a general stoney barrenness, and on the other side trees immediately begin, and it is Portugal and Devon that, happily, have the trees.

Devon has much else to recommend it — sharp climatic differences for one thing. To be relaxed, perhaps on holiday after a tense time in the City cornering jute or whatever, it is for South Devon that you should make and for the croquet-hoops of Budleigh Salterton, or Seaton, where the sensible Romans had seaside villas, or the beautiful valley and the red cliffs of Sidmouth where Queen Victoria had her first view of the briny. She came as a small child and was carried to the beach by her father, the impecunious Duke of Kent, travelling on borrowed money and pursued by his creditors. She returned later to the area in more affluent circumstances as Queen and, from the royal yacht, painted a charming water-colour picture of Torquay, the town where, of all weird places to choose, Kipling learnt to bicycle.

To be braced, head for the rugged North coast. I spent much of my childhood prodding about for living things among the fascinating sea-water pools of Ilfracombe and, on its shingle beaches, splashing in the icy waves that come rolling in from the Bristol Channel, aware that when the invigorating dip was over, there would be plates of what we called cut-rounds, a type of scone smothered in the richest Devonshire cream and home-made strawberry jam, waiting to be eaten in my grandfather's garden, which had a trout stream running through it and was surrounded by those entrancing fuchsia hedges.

Sometimes, as a change from the shingle, it was decided to spend the day to the South-West and on the sandy shores of Woolacombe. Private cars were then relatively rare and so parties were made up and a communal char-à-banc was hired, a vehicle with rather primitive rows of wooden seats and which quickly became, to an English tongue, a charabang and was later glorified into the modern 'coach'. Woolacombe was then a wilderness of sand-dunes in which we disrobed for bathing. Having recently seen *The Desert Song* at Drury Lane, I had a fantasy that any moment Harry Welchman would appear as the Red Shadow, on horseback and at the head of his wild desert tribe, the Riffs, all loudly singing that number that went: 'Ho! So we sing as we are riding, Ho! That's the time you'd best be hiding!' Similarly, viewing recently the telly production of *Churchill and the Generals*, I could swear that the scenes which purported to show them in North Africa, were actually shot at Woolacombe and, what is more, in front of a dune that I used to know.

Scenically Devon really has it all ways, the coast and the hinterland being of equal beauty. I have never much cared for great lumps of hill unadorned by trees. You get these huge mounds in Berkshire and Dorset where the residents, poor things, call them 'downs'. 'Who will o'er the downs so free?'

Not I, for a start. Nor do I greatly like the mountains with which they are so widely burdened up in Scotland. (Who was it who complained that the trouble with mountains was that they blocked the view?) But in Devon our high places are of the right size and shape, they cover themselves with heather and trees and valleys and ponies and wild life and they call themselves Dartmoor and Exmoor.

To the world at large, Dartmoor merely means either a prison or the place where Sherlock Holmes ('You know my methods, Watson') tracked down the Hound of the Baskervilles which was causing such consternation in and around the Great Grimpen Mire. But to those of us who live near it, Dartmoor is a place of enchantment and where, if your luck is in, you can see a flight of Canadian Geese come sweeping in to touch down on the waters of the Fernworthy reservoir, and where you can picnic on the slopes of Hay Tor (and it's a mistaken kindness to share things with the ponies) and, if it is a clear day, see the whole coastline, more or less, from Exmouth to Brixham.

When I was young, a friendly uncle, hoping to interest me, though Heaven knows why, in botany, presented me with a book that listed all the things that 'a lively youngster' might be able to hunt down and collect on Dartmoor. Such odd names! In the field of plants there were Bog Stitchwort, Scentless Feverfew, Depressed Feather Moss, Frog Orchis and a sad little growth called Small Quaking Grass. There was also Wild Thyme which I liked as I had shortly before seen a musical comedy in which the heroine sang: 'I'm very fond of Wild Thyme', to which her gentleman companion crisply replied: 'And I like a wild time too!' Impossible also not to smile when confronted by a couple of plants called Wild Basil and Hairy Violet. But I was no biologist and could take or leave such things as Adder's Tongue and Little Prickly Sedge.

Dartmoor too means to some people Old Uncle Tom Cobbleigh and all. One would, I think, have hardly cared to be Tom Pearse's old grey mare, doomed to carry such a fright-

106

ful collection of people (Dan'l Whiddon and Harry Hawk always sound especially off-putting), and subsequently to collapse and die from strain. But the church at Widecombe-in-the-Moor, struck by a jumbo fireball in 1638 during evening service (sixty-two worshippers badly damaged) but since restored, has much to recommend it. Its patron saint is St Pancras, a name which makes most of us look at our watches, quicken our step and wonder whether the four-fifteen will leave on time.

There's just so much else — the beautiful Exe valley, the anchorages under Berry Head where the pirates used to lurk, the splendours of Exeter cathedral, Brixham fishing boats, the gabled houses at Topsham where the Dutch merchants settled, people who say 'slummick' when they mean 'shamble' and 'popple-stones' when they mean 'pebbles' and 'mizzy-maazy' when they mean 'stupid', deer on Exmoor and the picturesque Brendon Valley of *Lorna Doone*, and the riverside cob and thatch houses of Bickleigh, where the salmon leap.

There are hundreds of lovely villages. There are cattle in rich pasture on the hills whichever way you care to look. The rivers are enchanting. (And who has ever seen an ugly river?) There is red earth and tiny winding lanes and there has never been such a place for primroses. It takes, of course, a little time to be accepted by those whose families have lived here for centuries. Villagers tend at first to be politely careful and distant in their relationships with 'vurriners'. I have lived in Devon for thirty-five years now and, three years ago, I was kindly invited to open the Church Fête (proceeds, as so often, for Repairs to the Roof). I had arrived.

RURAL MATTERS

Keen gardeners will not be surprised to learn that in the spacious grounds of 'Myrtlebank', August has seen much bustle and activity. The dahlias, that most showy and rewarding flower, have been better than ever this year but have needed, in this driest of dry months, watering. Ours live out and come through even the worst winters in fine style. The roses have been, and still are, a mass of bud and blossom but have needed dead-heading and, of course, feeding (I can't recommend too highly a climber called Handel, their mauvish-pink and white flowers being the jolliest thing out). The hibiscus are, as usual, admired by all but one of them, over-heavy as it is with blooms, has developed a tipsy tilt and, lurching like some bleary-eyed reveller over one of the paths, has had to be staked back. You'll want to know, in your friendly way, about our weeds. Doing just fine!

Dry leaves still lingering in the lane have finally been swept up and, together with, from the ditch, a splendid black liquid mulch formed of dead vegetation and goodness knows what, have been placed upon the compost heap. Mr Bricknell's sedate flock of elderly sheep have been keeping the orchard grass down and making the eventual apple-picking easier (we've already started on the Epicures — eaters — and the Rev Wilkes — cookers). There is an aged ram among the sheep who, remembering his golden youth and wondering whether the old skill is still there, occasionally tries a friendly approach to one of the flock and secures the chilliest of receptions ('Don't worry me now, Walter'). To the considerable envy of almost everybody else, we have got a fine crop of apples.

Next year's excitement (it is always 'next year' in a garden) is to be a new heather bed. Some roses that have never done well at the base of a rocky slope are to be moved and will leave a sunny space which, heavily peated, will welcome the heathers. Sun and rock should remind them of the moors and their natural habitat. They will be within sight of the sitting-room window and I can keep a sharp eye on them. There are those, though not I, who swear that growing things react well to a shout of 'I say, *do* buck up!' I'm getting more accustomed now to moving plants about. If they don't look happy, shift them. Just like you and I, some prefer what for them amounts to Scarborough rather than Frinton. And for others, Yarmouth is the favourite spot. I have a daphne that looks suicidal and so I am going to give it what in my garden is the equivalent of Dr Brighton.

Various considerations made it impossible to take this year our normal holiday in Amalfi and one of the considerations was that I had been honoured by being made this year's President of the Appleton and District Horticultural and Agricultural Society and the day of the fifty-second Annual Show fell slap in the middle of holiday time. Never mind, for it was a splendid affair altogether, which several lively meetings in the village hall had preceded. One of the economically advantageous items at a show is the Draw Tickets (for various prizes). At one of our meetings, the dear lady, no longer in the first flush of youth, who has been running, with willing volunteers, the selling of Draw Tickets for the last twenty years, attempted very tentatively to withdraw from her task. No hope at all and she was gently and politely shunted back into it, a despairing smile on her face showing everybody that she had had, from the first, no hope whatever of succeeding in her bid for freedom. In most villages and when somebody takes on a job, it is assumed ('The floral arrangements are, as ever, in the capable hands of Mrs Bowsher') that they will continue with it until they drop.

One of the major attractions at our show this year was the presence, deftly piloted by the owner from a neighbouring village, of a helicopter, not one of those vast ones which lug whole platoons of soldiers about but a slim two-seater with blades that looked barely adequate for their task of hoisting. There it stood just below the main field and looking somewhat out of place among our beautiful Devon hills. At an early meeting it was decided that the chief prize in the Draw should be 'A Ride in the Helicopter', either to Exeter or, should aerial traffic in that area be heavy, then over the Haldon hills and away for a peep at Torquay. Upon which a faint voice from the back of the hall asked how much one would have to pay *not* to go up in the helicopter (laughter, in which the President joined).

On the day itself we were all astir from an early hour. Hopeful winners of prizes duly carried down to the huge marquee, from eight a.m. onwards, and laid out on the trestle tables their entries for 'Vase of Five Rose Blooms with their Natural Foliage', 'Decorated Miniature Garden', 'Five Pieces Gingerbread', 'Pot of Lemon Curd' and 'Flower Gift for Friend in Hospital'. They were soon joined by the optimistic growers of vegetables bearing 'Five Sticks Rhubarb', 'Longest Kidney Bean', 'Three Beetroots Round', 'Three Beetroots Long', 'Two Cabbages, White' and 'Two Indoors Cucumbers'. Elsewhere other attractions were being made ready for inspection — Two Longwool Ewes, Two Fat Lambs, Heavy Horse, Female Kid over Two Months, Dog and Owner Most Alike, for which there is always a big entry, and Happiest Dog (ditto).

There was so much else — tugs of war, ladies' egg-and-spoon race, cross country race, mounted potato race, various classes of ponies, best turned-out horse in working harness, sheaf pitching competitions, and so on. The sun shone throughout. There was everywhere happiness and achievement. Spirits rose and one felt that, after all and despite the mounting horrors, all might, in the end, be well again with England.

BY YOUR FRUITS

Bad news from Appleton. The hornets have been at our plums.

Tiring of a purely apple diet (a brand of mid-season flowering cooker called the Rev W. Wilkes has been a special favourite with them), they swiftly switched a fortnight ago to the Czar plums which were just coming into delicious purple ripeness. My humane view in matters affecting the animal, bird and insect world, not to speak of the balance of nature and so on, has always been 'share and share alike', and for this reason we have always retained in the spacious grounds of 'Myrtlebank' a specimen or two of forsythia, though seldom a blossom do we see for the buds are the particular joy of the beautiful bullfinches who nip them off with lively enjoyment as soon as they appear. And we have a few nut-trees but mainly for the benefit of a charming little grey squirrel (yes, yes, I know how naughty they are) who hops about and climbs here and there and appears to be domiciled in a bijou penthouse perched in a tallish poplar, a dwelling obviously boasting a well-stocked and nut-filled larder.

I regret to have to tell you, however, that hornets are by nature determinedly egomaniac and simply do not understand what is meant by sharing. Their peevish and belligerent attitude to anybody attempting to pick a plum leaves a great deal to be desired and so, to teach them a sharp lesson, we suspend beneath the trees jam-jars the tops of which are covered by a paper lid with a slight perforation in it through which the hornets can penetrate but out through which they find it difficult to back-track. To entice them into the jars, we fill them (the jars) with a heady mixture of beer and jam whose aroma mounts and encircles the plums and lures the marauders down. You'll want to know the composition of our mélange. We find that a blend of either Worthington's pale ale or Charrington's best bitter, coupled with a generous dollop of strawberry jam (Tiptree, naturally), works splendidly. The hornets hasten to abandon the fruit, hurry on down and into the jars, become rapidly intoxicated (in its way such a tribute to our fine British beers), sink into the liquid and drown, but what a lively way to go. When my time comes, pray prepare for me a joyous tub of Double Diamond and Tiptree (the Morello Cherry Conserve, if you can run to it) and just dump me in.

All those deeply concerned with theological matters will have been scratching their tonsures and wondering about the Rev W. Wilkes, relished by hornets and whom, as you will recall, I mentioned in connection with nutritious cooking apples. W for Walter, William, Wilfred or Wilberforce, do you suppose, and how did it come about that an ordinary Rev got an apple, albeit merely a humble cooker, named after him, a feat never achieved even by the saintliest of Bishops? Perhaps, intrigued by fruit, he was able to snatch a precious moment or two away from font and pulpit to dabble in the orchard with grafting and root-pruning and all that. I see him as a rather pallid bachelor with, and how rightly, a prominent Adam's apple, his sole physical attraction a rather flutey tenor voice and a little inclined to preach sermons with texts such as 'Blessed are the meek' and 'Offer him the other cheek'. Not a robust type. This picture that I have of him is suggested by the fact that, or so my gardening book informs me, the Rev W. Wilkes is 'self-sterile' and requires a vigorous cross-pollinator which flowers at a similar period to get the Rev Wilkes, so to speak, going. Although I hereby run the risk of getting this horticultural divine unfrocked, I must state another fact, namely that the cross-pollinator especially recommended to cope with the Rev's troubles is none other than our old friend, Laxton's Superb, a sturdy and virile apple if ever there was one. The whole proceeding, linking together as it does wet Wilkes and lusty Laxton, seems to me to smack rather too much of some of the activities discussed at such length in the Wolfenden Report. I may be, and indeed am, unduly sensitive but the first four letters of the word hornet are a worry too.

My gardening book was published in 1930 and shows the Rev W. Wilkes to have been already an apple of repute at that date, nearly fifty years ago. He can surely hardly have had an apple named after him while he was still a pale young curate, entrusted with an occasional and sparsely-filled evening service or the odd Churching of Women (a brisk affair lasting at the most fifteen minutes), and the distinction must have come to him when 'of riper years', a phrase I use purposely and in admiration of this excellent yellowish cooking apple. It seems therefore more than likely that the Rev W. Wilkes has passed across by now and learnt the answer to the Great Riddle, but should he be by any chance still happily with us and the life and soul of the Clergymen's Rest Home, let me assure him that I am speaking of him solely in his apple persona. And let me remind him that when the late Godfrey Winn had a rose named after him, he did not at all mind being announced to the world as costing seven shillings and sixpence and requiring a good mulch at frequent intervals. And he allowed himself to appear, complete with rose and house and toupet, on a coloured tea-towel of which I am very happy to have an example.

A thing of beauty is a joy forever, as the poet Keats so correctly reminds us, and Godfrey's luxuriant toupet was a constant delight and fascination to behold. It is only when Keats goes on to say that, with a thing of beauty, 'its loveliness increases', one feels that, in this particular case, the loveliness stayed right there where it was. Malcolm Muggeridge has described how it feels to appear with it, attached of course to its wearer, on the telly and how, when not in use, it sat snugly in a cardboard box and arrived by car. But whence came it? Sent by a fan? Lovingly pieced together from strands dropped and carefully gathered in the great youthful days? A postal bargain advertised in the Sundays? It was certainly not one of those beige teapot cosies which you sometimes see walking along streets on somebody's head and which announce themselves as being false from a distance of eighty yards. It tended down the years to cover a necessarily larger area and to advance and recede like the waves of the sea. Sometimes it hovered in mid-crumpet. Sometimes it withdrew and stayed modestly back from the crown. Sometimes, in a sort of defiant gesture, it plunged forward over the forehead and nearly joined up with the eyebrows. I got into terrible trouble once (on the grounds, as usual and as here, perhaps, of Bad Taste) for saying that two of the titles of the three volumes planned, but not fully completed, of his autobiography revealed that the works were, in point of fact, a disguised history of Godfrey's hair. The titles were *The Infirm Glory* and *Here Is My Space*. Well, what else could one possibly think? Never mind. He brought pleasure to millions (remember his Cudlipp-invented Personality Parade in the *Daily Mirror* in the '30s?) and his rose lives on.

Prior to 1930, and since then for all I know, ladies were far from well represented in the fruit world. There was certainly an apple called Annie Elizabeth ('good firm flesh') but then she might be just anybody. There was Lady Sudeley who showed her grip on things by liking to be cross-pollinated by a Cox's Orange Pippin, and among gooseberries we find Broom Girl (described as having 'very large fruits') who was obviously a well-favoured member of some household staff. There is a mid-season pear called Louise Bonne of Jersey who must, like all pears, be caught for eating at just the right ripe moment: delay another hour or two and all is lost (*what* a tricky fruit).

I am afraid that it is the more successful kinds of men who hog the orchard limelight, with the Duke of Devonshire and

Lords Derby, Grosvenor and Lambourne, not to speak of Prince Albert himself. Dreadful old Gladstone appears twice, first as a very far from self-sterile mid-season pippin and again, and could anything be less suitable, as a late peach. Sir Joseph Paxton has been rightly and fittingly honoured among the strawberries. Biblical characters have not been neglected (there is a splendidly fruity black currant called Goliath, there are Saints Edmund and Everard) and Prince Albert crops up again amongst the red currants. Two delightful finds: first, among the raspberries, of all places to put him, there is the Hailsham Berry (autumn fruiting, and very nice too) and then, among the 'perpetual fruiting' strawberries, there is the world's most mysterious Saint, St Fiacre. How he comes to be connected with those terrifying Paris taxis, Heaven alone knows.

ON YOUR MARKS

I have sometimes wondered, in that spare ten minutes before my toad-in-the-hole has risen and assumed what some cookery articles refer to as 'crispy brownness', what would have happened if the *Titanic*, instead of striking that iceberg a glancing, though fatal, blow had simply gone absolutely full tilt into it. Would it have split the berg, sunk like a stone, exploded, crumpled up like a concertina or ridden up onto the ice and then toppled over sideways? A marine engineer or a ships' designer could, I suppose, give me some idea and I hope one day to bump into one such who can fill me in. I just throw the matter out as a *pensée*.

Sitting happily here in Devon and pondering, as is my way, on this and other of the really important things of life — the deteriorating quality of your average doughnut, whether dear Mrs Thatcher ever finds time for 'elevenses', the lethal nature or not of butter, and why all ex-prime ministers save one wear the same woebegone look of undertakers who in a profession-ally thin year have come to measure up for the coffin — I placidly ask myself whether it is verbally possible to be the very opposite of overwrought, namely underwrought.

Naturally, I drop everything and hasten at once to my *Chambers*, a name evocative both for barristers and for schoolboys of fifty years ago ('Please, Matron, I've cracked my chamber'), and what do I find? There is 'underwrought' as large as life, even though, as the past tense of underwork, it is only found in *Shak.* and is therefore labelled *obs.* My *Chambers Twentieth Century Dictionary* is, I don't need to tell you, the very latest and up-to-the-minute edition (1972) and boasts (by which I mean 'speaks proudly of') the very newest and highly specialised meanings of some words that I don't really much care about, such as capsule, dish, gutsy, kitsch and viable. And there is quite a lot of slang included — drop out, hang-up, uptight and whizz-kid, all words which here in this column make their first and last appearance, together with the, to me, totally unacceptable phrase which goes: 'I had a gut reaction.' At all events and from now on in, it is to be underwrought and unworked up that I am aiming at. No more flying off the handle. No more tetchy cries of 'Bother!' A new serenity is to be mine.

And it is in this mood of quiet acceptance that I recently wrote (no replies yet but these things take time) to my old friend of Cambridge days, Lord Killanin, and various others, offering our Devon village of Appleton for at least part of the next Olympics, that part that concerns long-distance running or walking in stiffish and exacting conditions, and in all weathers. I have not yet approached our parish council about it but they are a charming assortment of elected residents of long standing and they would, I am confident, jump at the idea (and here, clutching my *Chambers* again, I hastily point out that I use the verb 'jump at' in the sense of 'accept with eagerness' rather than 'start with fright at', as in 'Goodness me, *how* she jumped!'). And the venue is in every way suitable. There are high hills for the hardy to run up and, subsequently, down. There are streams to leap and fords to ford and our Marathon would really be worthy of the name. To celebrate the Jubilee, a new room was added on to our already commodious village hall, the new addition being called, after some anxious thought, the 'Jubilee Room', and so there is heaps of space for the athletes to tog up in (obsessed with words as I have now become, I am asking myself what on earth the opposite of 'tog up' can be. Neither 'tog down' nor 'tog off' sounds quite right, or very nice).

As to accommodation at nightfall, I see in my mind's eye a tented enclosure down by the valley road and convenient for the River Teign and that healthful morning plunge. And as

Right Prep school days – dressed for the camera.

Below Cambridge days – dressed for the stage.

Stealing the show?

Oundle school staff. Arthur still holds centre stage.

At the time of his first radio broadcast.

On Active Service.

With Leslie Phillips and Terry Thomas, in the south of France.

At the controls of an Inter-City 125 train.

Call My Bluff, with Frank Muir and Robert Robinson.

All Star Secrets, with Michael Parkinson.

With Prunella Scales, raising funds for
the Arts Theatre, Cambridge.

At a *Yorkshire Post* book signing.

At 'Myrtlebank'.

In the garden.

On holiday in Florida with Peter Kelland.

Indian Summer – dressed for the
camera.

for food, Miss Entwhistle's *cuisine* is, and rightly, much admired for the exotic nature of its dishes (her stuffed cabbage Tahiti-style has been quite a local talking point for some time) and she would be fully equal to the challenge of providing, for those foreigners who cannot face life without them, such delicacies as borscht and pumpernickel and pumpkin pie. The Bultitudes, who spend so much of their time abroad, should be able to rattle off greetings in numerous foreign tongues, though I rather fear that they may regard it as being solely a fun occasion and go around waving bottles and shrieking: 'Cheerioski!' I aim myself to be present at every event save that of fast walking which I regard as being the most idiotic and ugly form of competitive athletics ever invented, with the poor body seen to be crying out in protest every inch of the way and just longing to break into a trot.

After some consideration, and with the nation's best interests at heart, I have decided not to allow my name to be put forward for any of the events here. I do not at all like walking in any case, and my running is, I am afraid, rather rusty for I have not been anywhere called on to run competitively since 1926. In common with many houses in public schools, my house at Oundle possessed a silver cup donated by an Old Boy (who knows from what sadistic impulse?) for local speediness and for which everybody under the age of sixteen had to compete in a road race round a charming village called Ashton, a locality made famous originally by a branch of the Rothschild family who lived there and had advanced and philanthropic ideas about the improvement of village life, and more recently by the World Conker Championship which is held there. However, none of these delights did we have time to savour as we flashed past, some of us flashing rather more rapidly than others. The distance run was, I suppose, about two miles and to get us going there was no nonsense about starting-blocks: just a brief Ready-Steady-GO!, and away we went. As the event took place immediately after lunch, it was somewhat taxing for the more sensitive digestions, digestions already taking the strain and at full stretch after the lunch itself. The first boy home, though doubtless preferring some

119

more tangible reward in the shape of cash or a hamper of tuck, had the honour of having his name inscribed on the cup, an honour denied, alas, to me. There were, I think, about thirty of us running and perhaps you'll like to know where I finished up. Two from last, and to cries of 'Run up!' from the few spectators who had not already dispersed.

But although I prefer on this occasion to hide my light under what really needs to be only a very small bushel, I shall not be inactive for I plan to move freely about among the competitors dispensing advice, encouragement (dear old 'Run up!' again) and information, the last being garnered from a splendid book, Dr Gardiner's *Athletics of the Ancient World* and a positive little gold-mine of fascinating nuggets of, presumably, fact. Pinning to myself a notice saying AVAILABLE IN THREE LANGUAGES, the other two being French and German, I hope to stun one and all.

Although boxing doesn't, in my view, rate very highly as an athletic activity, had you ever realised that, according to Homer, when a fight was set up between Odysseus (disguised for plot purposes as a beggar) and a genuine beggar called Irus, the purse was a haggis? Odysseus won the tasty trophy by what was obviously a foul blow behind the ear (in course of time, the haggis was removed and a crown of bay-leaves substituted, to the dismay of the peckish). Odysseus then goes on to take part in some rather showy wrestling, a vase drawing of 430 BC showing the kind of thing that they used to get up to and which nowadays would mean instant arrest and closure of the hall. Discoveries in Greece reveal a sandstone block weighing half a ton, lifted with one hand (follow that!) by Bybon and tossed over his head. And as to diet, the athlete Milo, tuning up for Olympia, munched for supper a four-year-old heifer, lightly browned on both sides.

And so on and so forth. I've heaps more to tell and so do look out for me. I'll be near, if not actually in, the Refreshment Tent.

BLOSSOM TIME

How little it takes to shake the self-confidence of even somebody as complacent as I. Until about a fortnight ago my life here in Devon was running smoothly, although I do not see myself as possessing pistons, flywheels, cylinders and slide-valves, like a well-oiled machine. 'Myrtlebank' was in all its early summer glory, its great south front ablaze with wistaria, clematis and climbing roses. The four clumps of arum lilies (don't be envious of me but they flourish finely here) are out (and I go into the present tense for they still are) and provide a real joy to the eye. Various pink and yellow rock plants are hard at it (the pasque-flowers were better than ever this year and all were fully a-bloom, as usual, in time for Easter) and any moment now the campanulas that cling to my low stone walls will be bursting into bluish-mauve splendour. The may trees, three in number (there used to be five but we had to say good-bye to the two that had flourished too violently and were removing too much light, air and sunshine) are in gorgeous flower, two pink, one red. The numerous fuchsias, all of which defy the worst that the winter can arrange for them, are shooting vigorously up. The three rose-beds, heavily dunged at an early date, show buds galore and, although green-fly are unsightly and unacceptable, the little beasts never seem to do really serious damage to the actual flowers. In sum, an idyllic scene, *n'est-ce pas*? (and I here dwindle into Frog for a reason that will shortly be apparent and to prepare you for what is to come).

And it is not only in the garden that everything, until those two weeks ago, was lovely. Appleton, our village, was its customary happy self, with tea-parties here and whist drives there and, for we are an unusually generous community, little presents of deep-frozen this and home-made that changing hands. Miss Entwhistle, enterprising as ever, is said to have made a lightning dash by rail (day trip and cheap fare, if cheap it may truly be called) to Oxford Street, which is still the Mecca of fashion as far as we are concerned, and to have returned with several startling new confections, and the phrase about mutton being dressed as lamb is hovering on some people's lips. (And whatever, incidentally, became of mutton, mutton chops being in many ways far more succulent than lamb? What about boiled mutton and caper sauce? Legs of lamb don't work nearly as well. Possibly the lambs that are currently being refused elsewhere could be allowed to grow, reach seniority and become mutton.) Canon Mountjoy reports that Berenice (Mrs Mountjoy) has quite recovered from her fall, which was not, I hasten to say and perish the thought, a fall from grace but a clumsy tumble over a flower-pot and a mishap that might happen to anybody. She can now, hooray, put both feet to the ground and Matins is once more a possibility.

We are at the moment without cocktail parties — no great hardship to me, as I can take them or leave them alone — our cocktail-providers, the Bultitudes, having left Heidelberg, whence came *post-karten* which I regret to say spoke disparagingly of those who, to Giles, will for ever be Krauts, and being now in, surprise surprise, Cannes, whence also come *cartes postales* usually penned in Bunty's flowing fist (about three words to a line), making much mention of 'dos' on Laddy's yacht and kindly suggesting, as is her way, that the whole of Appleton should fly out and join them. Even if fully restored to mobility, I do not somehow see Berenice Mountjoy 'crewing' for Laddy.

It is typical of our dear village that (for they are fairly recent arrivals) we were able to absorb the Bultitudes and their relatively wild and exotic goings-on without a hiccough, for their hearts are so very much in the right place and they are loved by all. That is the key. Who minds shrieks of 'Whack-oh!' and 'Cheerybung!' when they come from such a kind, warm pair? An alarming tale is told of a neighbouring village in which a married couple from the Midlands decided to settle, and who were, plainly, unacceptable and in the wrong spot — snooty (if for once I may use such a vulgar word), stingy, cold and pleased with themselves. Two old residents were heard discussing them in the village shop, one of whom let fall the ominous phrase: 'Us'll get rid of they.' It took them, it seems, slightly less than a year.

But to my jolt. The Bultitudes are not great readers at any time and, even though currently in France, I rather doubt whether they dip very often into the thoughtful work of René Descartes and his *Le Discours de la Méthode*. He was *né*, I hardly need to remind you, in 1596, and *mort* fifty-four years later, and he gave out *pensée* after *pensée*, some of which, or so I gather from my *Oxford Book of Quotations*, were regrettably in Latin. I say regrettably because of the years of horror, misery and boredom inflicted by that dreadful tongue on countless generations of schoolboys. When one even faintly complained to those in authority, the answer was a parrot cry of either: 'Oh, it will help you with your English,' or 'Oh, it will help you to think logically.' Take your choice. The pitiful results are before you. There were various replies possible to these faulty assertions and I will choose the most seemly of them. 'Rubbish!' However, and be that as it may, René's most popular *pensée* was, undoubtedly, *Cogito, ergo sum*, which readily translates itself into Frog as *Je pense, donc je suis* or in English as 'I think, therefore I exist', a *pensée* with which nobody has ever dreamt of quarrelling. My present trouble is that there is now doubt about *qui*, or 'who', *je suis*. Here is what befell me.

Old men certainly forget, and what they chiefly forget is what they told you five minutes ago and which they are happily in the process of telling you all over again, and so I therefore apologise if I have made constant previous mention of a, for me, enjoyable year when I was called in by my old friend, Hugh, or 'Binkie', Beaumont, the dazzlingly successful head of the theatrical firm of H.M. Tennent, to assist in the London production of a play called *Cactus Flower*, a French piece which originated triumphantly in Paris, then appeared, translated, in New York and which was now due for London, where the very American text had to be altered to suit English audiences, and this was the delightful task allotted to me.

All for me was *couleur de rose*. Our stars were Margaret Leighton and Tony Britton, that charmingly gifted and sensitive light comedian. Our theatre was the Lyric, its stage possessing what is called 'a revolve' (I never did tire of standing in the wings and watching the sets whirring round during the theatrical black-outs). And our American director was a splendidly bouncy and vigorous and experienced and efficient man of the stage and films and called Abe Burrows, who, although hotly contesting some of the many verbal changes that I had made in his script, was friendly, and we got on well. He chose to regard me as being a typically English museum piece (fairly true, even then — it was 1967) and he went off into screeches of merry laughter when I chanced to mention my club in Pall Mall or some similar institution. But he was too polite to mock one unkindly and for the six weeks that we rehearsed and at frequent intervals during the seven months that we played and until Miss Leighton, previously committed, had to leave and go to New York, we had endless discussions and conferences and became, or so I felt, chummy colleagues. He was nice enough to wish me, while he was directing, to be ever at his side, and he looked about for me if I wasn't there (I once had to go to the BBC, a word which at once had him in stitches).

Abe has now written his autobiography, published in America but not yet here, I understand, where his name means not a great deal to the reading public. And it is not the only name to lack impact for a fortnight ago, a friend who has read the book informed me that, when referring kindly to the London production of *Cactus Flower*, he says that he was helped in the enterprise 'by a friend of Binkie's called Arthur Blossom'. Did you ever! What is one to make of it? For all those thirteen years I have been hanging about in the Burrows mind as 'Blossom'. To him, *je suis* Blossom. Well, I suppose it could have been a lot worse.

SUNDAY BEST

VERY IMPORTANT PLEASURES

My dear old cousin Madge, who breasted Life's Finishing Tape at a very respectable ninety-three (I refer to years of age rather than to her mph), nursed in much earlier days a discreet passion for the charming musical comedy star of stars, Jack Buchanan.

Finding herself, around 1930 and rather improbably for her, in a party at the then fashionable Kitcat Nightclub, and excitedly perceiving that her idol was also there and upon the floor, she encouraged her dancing partner so to arrange their gyrations that they bumped heavily into Mr Buchanan, from which mishap conversation must surely arise.

It did indeed but apparently only of the tamest Consequences kind. He said to her: 'I beg your pardon.' She said to him: 'Our fault entirely.' The result was they never met again and the World said: 'Well, well!' Still, he had spoken to her and she to him, and that was something. And possibly she had upon her person a small bruise to treasure.

Somerset Maugham, whose thoughts did not always run along the cheeriest of lines, once announced that he had little patience with those who yearned to meet the great of this world, but he only announced it after he himself had met most of them and, his standards being high, had in general found them to be a disappointing lot. But then, as they say, he would, wouldn't he?

In this conflict of views I am entirely on the side of my cousin Madge. As a lifelong hero-worshipper myself, I am here to state that I have had nothing but happiness from the activity, surely the most selfless and outgoing of pastimes.

Occasional meetings with those one admired have seldom provided a let-down. As a boy at Oundle, I became, in due course and as a plaything of Nature, the possessor of an alto voice of astonishing power and startling resonance. We altos, we happy few, keen singers all, were well positioned for the school performance of *Messiah*, right to the fore and under the benevolent eyes of the sensational contralto soloist, Miss Margaret Balfour, befurred and bejewelled and given to mouthing: 'Wonderful, darlings!' at us when opportunity allowed. She was very approachable and loved to chat and we all adored her.

Schoolboys are quick to adopt and use a new catch-phrase and 'Wonderful, darlings!' became one of ours, especially when applied satirically. And thus it was that our house rugger team, returning after a shattering defeat, was greeted with loud cries of 'Wonderful, darlings!', words fatally overheard by the Victorian-minded and stuffy housemaster and resulting in the most frightful commotion ('What is the meaning of this odious and womanly form of salute?') requiring hours of patient explanation by the head of house.

But as to heroes, even Mr Maugham was vulnerable. I was present long ago at a small South of France lunch party which included Bunny Austin, our English tennis player then at the height of his fame. It was amusing to see our host, Mr Maugham, goggling away admiringly like the rest of us. Jolly to find a chink in that armour. Actually, rather heart-warming.

SUNNY SIDE UP

Those of us who live, and how happily, in remote Devon villages are apt to be regarded by the general public as being backward bumpkins, permanently astonished by modern wonderments such as Daz and the check-out points at Sainsbury's and for ever saying: 'Well oi'll be darned.'

Quite wrong, and I am glad to report the presence in our village of a solar panel, installed a few years ago by a splendidly go-ahead lady of fairly advanced years who, on fully clement days, proudly announced herself to be the possessor of a tankful of the hottest kind of bath water produced at nil expense. One imagined her sloshing away in an almost Roman and orgiastic splendour of steam and exotic bath salts. Beat that, Cheltenham!

Furthermore, we are always ready to cherish and revere fellow villagers who have distinguished themselves in some novel way and I recall a delightful woman resident, now alas no longer here below, who had a reputation for being a really tremendous globetrotter. There was almost nowhere, it was said, where she had not been and one had visions of her in Peru or Alaska or shinning up Everest until it was discovered that the most she had managed by way of travel was to go twice by train to Scarborough. Never mind. The dear creature has taken a longer trip since ('Hullo, Mozart!').

I have done my humble best for the village's reputation for modernity by becoming the owner of one of those miraculous watches that never need winding, and now it is oi who am indeed darned. It is not, I hasten to say, one of those watches that apparently get wound up by the owner just walking about for I do the minimum amount of walking about. I have always found unnecessary movement distasteful in the extreme and wasteful of energy and shoe leather. Those ghastly prep school compulsory crocodile walks are a hateful memory, until my friend, Williamson, coached me in how to feign a painfully twisted ankle, coupled with an ear-splitting: 'Ouch!'

My watch goes, I am told, by an electric battery of unimaginable smallness. It neither gains nor loses and remains in perfect step with those BBC pips and the tasteful male tones of the telephone's time announcer, though I rather prefer a soothing female voice to tell one a time that is almost always either earlier or later than one thought possible and therefore something of a shock.

And prominent among recent shocks was the information that at the end of 1987 we should all have added on an extra second (or was it take away a second?) because of galactic considerations or something equally incomprehensible. But what one could all too easily comprehend was the additional news that the earth is getting tired of rotating and *is slowing down*. Did you ever!

When it stops turning altogether, one so wants to know just exactly where would be the prudent place to take up residence. My thoughts turn naturally to Devon. Will palmy Torquay be pointing directly at the sun, do you suppose, and will therefore be able to offer permanent light and heat? One's electricity bills are a prime consideration here.

On the other hand, dawn is a very agreeable time of day. What about living in a continual dawn at, say, Paignton? Rather hard cheese, all this, on Australians but then they shouldn't live so far away.

And anyhow, Australians have had perfect sunny weather for two hundred years, more or less. It's our turn now.

RHAPSODIES

Have you ever noticed that, as is the way with earthquakes and tidal waves and typhoons, piano-tuners seem to turn up just when the fancy takes them, though they do make rather less of a disturbance?

Probably, and ages ago, a half-yearly date was agreed on, long since forgotten by the piano's owner. Piano-tuners are delightful men with a dedicated air and obviously a deep veneration for what some lightly call 'the ivories' and it is sad that they have to grow accustomed to discouraging front door receptions ('Oh blast! Our Mrs B was just going to do that room'), an incivility later assuaged by coffee and a plate of digestives.

The niceness of piano-tuners is only rivalled by that of furniture removers, an unfailingly cheerful and helpful body of men, apparently only too happy to dismantle the Bechstein and cart it down three narrow flights of stairs, followed by a rickety tallboy and a fairly awful water-colour of Paignton ('My mother's work. Exquisite, is it not? In her day she was quite a well known brush.')

Perhaps it is because tuners and removers are both bodies of men who come into the house and become temporarily members of the family, as it were. But then burglars do that, too. Incidentally, for every burglar at work there must be at least six people — friends, relations, neighbours — who are perfectly well aware what he (note the sex) is up to. If you happen to know any, do please go and tell them to stop it.

In my childhood we lived in London and possessed a grand

piano and I greatly enjoyed the tuner's visits for, after the repetitive plonks and twangs, he always ended with what was known as a *valse brillante*, a tremendous cascade of notes and a great flow of melody, hands all over the shop — a showy piece designed, I suppose, to test every re-twanged wire. I used to beg him for an encore, always graciously supplied (a flashy Chopin *étude*). Are tuners failed concert artistes? It is a thought too painful to dwell on.

The tuner had another attraction for me for one of the tools of his trade was piano-wire and this was well known to be what flew Peter Pan to and fro across the Darlings' night nursery; all that stuff about fairy dust and 'you just think lovely wonderful thoughts' was just so much twaddle. Indeed, a poorly handled limelight occasionally provided a quick glimpse of the wire positively in action. So there you are then!

When the Kaiser's zeppelins brought his so-called Reign, or Rain, of Terror to London (it was said to be composed of fifty-pound bombs tastefully hand-dropped from the gondola, with whatever is the German for 'Take that!'), my parents lovingly and wildly over-estimated my importance in the world and packed me off to my paternal grandmother, safely housed in Essex. She was what is known as 'musical', an excellent pianist with a charming voice, and we fell for each other hook, line and sinker.

Her tuner, jollity itself, and in imitation of the Frog composer Chaminade who wrote a piano piece for her four nieces, ran up a jolly number for the three of us, with a fairly simple treble section for me. We performed it at concerts for War charities. The applause was deafening and went straight to my head (with the still sadly visible results).

Who can doubt that the office of grandmother was especially invented by God as a reward for those who have endured and come safely through the countless and often painful disadvantages of motherhood?

BOY WHO WOULD BE KING

Even as old and full of information as I now am, I still find that almost every day some astounding new fact, hitherto unvouchsafed to me, pops up from nowhere to baffle and amaze. Wasn't it a Louis who constantly demanded ('*étonne-moi*') to be astonished? Well, I could have obliged him.

Glancing recently at a most reputable newspaper, I found it there authoritatively stated that the Russian word for God is Bog. Did you ever! I make no comment beyond the obvious one that, as names go, it doesn't come out as being particularly celestial, but then why should it?

It is not easy to rid oneself of the childhood idea of God — a whiskery old gentleman apt to get a bit ratty if crossed, permanently resident on clouds immediately overhead and just about five miles up. Whether or not this position denied the use of him to Australians, or whether they get him upside down, who can say?

At my prep school we had a new kind of God in the person of my friend Williamson. At first he contented himself with pretending that he was just a King, Henry VIII for preference, graciously living incognito amongst us. It was considered merry to rush up to him, bow low and then deliver some shattering piece of bad news, hoping to catch him off-guard. But then, tiring of regal rank, he took on a loftier mantle, moving serenely and Godlike among us, forgiving a sin here, bestowing a blessing there, and everywhere nodding approval of his own handiwork. Sometimes, quite carried away by his role, he would say Grace at lunch before the headmaster could

135

get the words out ('Leave the room, Williamson').

His speech, too, took colour from the new impersonation and became rich and reminiscent ('Wist ye not that I must go and do my prep?' and 'Whither thou goest, Miss Stacey, I will go too'), Miss Stacey being the Matron leading him off to the medicine cupboard for a hearty dose of the dreaded Gregory Powder. Williamson remained a card to the end and on his last day at the school insisted on giving leaving presents to the entire domestic staff, an unheard of outburst of generosity. Not for him the anti-tipping brigade that appears to be currently alive.

In which connection I recall the unusual case of an almost Dickensian warm-heartedness concerning the London club of which I am a happy member. In 1946 a sharply worded notice from the secretary reminded us all that the club rules forbade any tipping of servants. Upon which a fellow member and friend of mine, resenting the reminder and its cheerless tone, summoned as many club servants as he could find and, passing along the line, handed to each a five pound note with the words: 'Please don't tell the Committee or I shall have to resign.' Naughty but kind, and nobody blabbed.

He had indeed to resign later on but for a different reason. You may care to know his name. It was Guy Burgess. I am indeed glad to rescue from oblivion the memory of a sunny deed from among a number of other deeds that were considerably less acceptable.

QUICK MARCH TO
MATRON'S ROOM

I am afraid that both the Armed Forces Minister and the Chairman of the WRVS have got it all wrong. It is neither agony aunts, too sentimental by half, nor mother-substitutes that the Army requires to cope with the problems of young soldiers. The ideal person is already available, hard at work elsewhere and well trained and in full supply — the school matron. If you doubt her capabilities in this field, ask the nearest schoolmaster.

For one thing she is medically experienced and able to help the MO in minor matters. Picture the scene. A private soldier, damaged on a route march, arrives limping at her sitting-room door, to be met with: 'Come in, dear, and let me have a peep at that troublesome old groin of yours.' The deft and Barts-trained fingers prod and soothe and meanwhile the gas-fire hisses comfortingly, a pussy-cat purrs on the hearth-rug and a vase of nasturtiums stands brightly on the window-sill. All matrons instantly and effectively create a home atmosphere. Then: 'Do I see someone who can manage a cup of cocoa? Sit ye down by that plate of digestives that badly needs attention by somebody not a mile from here.' Sip, sip and munch, munch. And then: 'Tell me all about yourself, Colin. It is Colin, isn't it? I thought I saw you looking the wee-est bit downhearted after grenade throwing.' And out pour all the troubles — the homesickness, the rough talk, the some-times harsh treatment, and eventually a Name is provided. Matron's lips tighten. 'Send him to me the moment tank drill is over. No, I won't split on him to Major Bulstrode, but I wouldn't care to be in that man's shoes when I get at him.'

Let it not for a moment be thought that school matrons are a soft touch. Far from it. I once heard a matron say, in an outraged voice: 'You dare to come to me with a wretched little sprained thumb and the house match final tomorrow! Be off with you!' Just substitute 'manoeuvres' for 'housematch final' and you find yourself with a full complement of men.

A further advantage. By the very nature of their job they tend to be emotionally unencumbered by anything in trousers. Lavish affection is poured out on their charges but otherwise they remain heartwhole. They make do with very little accomodation. They seldom require days off ('I'll just nip over to Boots on my bike. We're right out of petroleum jelly').

The matrons I have known have all been pleasantly conversational and keen on a gossip, which would provide an added amenity for a recruit longing to talk to somebody sympathetic about his girlfriend. So, after the assault course, Colin turns up again. Matron is all attention. 'Oh, so this is a snap of Miss Wright, is it, the great Christine? What a very charming face! And such a pretty smile. I expect she takes after her mother, girls usually do, luckily for them, ha, ha. And that's Tiger, I suppose, all ready for his din-din. You are a lucky fellow. But then she is too.'

Before long we may well have her running the whole place, with recruits asking anxiously: 'Please, Matron, is it clean socks tomorrow?'

ON THE ROAD TO COTTERSTOCK

I was a schoolmaster for twenty-three years, the war inter-
vening, and used sometimes, when exhaustion reigned and
spirits were low, to envy the carefree attitude of a young
master at a sister foundation.

Arriving on the Friday to teach Divinity and Woodwork, he
disappeared totally from view and was next seen early on the
Sunday morning lying dead drunk in a pigsty behind the
chapel. Apart from being conveniently placed for Matins, his
situation had little to recommend it from a professional point
of view.

At Oundle I did once see, after our morning Harvest
Festival service, one of our older chaplains emerging somewhat furtively from the vestry and clutching a brown paper
bag. It had the look of being a paper bag that contained a
pound or so of cooking apples. He saw me watching him and
scuttled off.

However, when at the end of Evensong I examined the
autumnal fruit display, I could spot no gap in the apple
section. Perhaps, on the way home, the priest had had a Road
to Damascus experience, though in his case it would have been
the Road to Cotterstock, and had been guided to return the
apples under cover of the *Nunc Dimittis*.

At school we had periodically to endure the *Benedicite* sung in
full. In case your memory of this Canticle is rusty, it is the one
that requires a series of improbable things to praise the Lord
and magnify Him for ever. It is all, quite frankly, dreadful
twaddle and how on earth can you magnify somebody who,

one would have thought, is already quite sufficiently magnified?

A hearty school matron of my acquaintance used to express her inability to perform some task or other with the phrase: 'No can do.' It is a suitable motto for the *Benedicite*, for among the things that would experience difficulty when called upon to praise the Lord we find Dews (twice mentioned), Frosts, Whales, Wells, Winds, Ice, Snow and Floods, the last named being guilty down the years of causing endless disasters and being a most unsuitable inclusion.

'All that move in the waters' is mentioned and presumably embraces those sardines not yet in tins and those pilchards not yet in tomato sauce, but does it include summer bathers at, say, Shanklin? They certainly move vigorously in the waters, nobody more so. Perhaps Dr Runcie would give us a ruling here. One doesn't want to go wasting praise quite needlessly. And I do rather wonder about a God who appears to need such constant buttering up (no religious pamphlets, please).

However and be all that as it may, I am perfectly ready to give praise and thanks for everything that makes my life such a happy one — food processor, electric razor, P.G. Wodehouse and chicken liver risotto lightly dusted with Parmesan.

Perhaps there is Something (or Somebody) in it after all.

GIRLS WILL BE BOYS

The exciting announcement in the papers this week that Oundle School is to go co-educational may well have led some readers to think that this great and progressive establishment has for once been caught lagging behind.

Not at all, for where many public schools have merely inserted some hand-picked seventeen-year-olds into their sixth forms — which represents just a feeble dabbling with the subject — Oundle is dealing with the challenge on an altogether grander scale. Two new boarding houses are to be built for the accommodation of girls from age thirteen upwards; so Oundle is again well to the fore in the educational field and hang the expense.

Various interesting points instantly present themselves. Is the ultimate aim to have equal numbers of boys and girls? How soon and in what proportion would the common-room become mixed and is there the distinct possibility of a future headmistress of Oundle?

Then what are the girls to be *called*? Schoolboys are traditionally known by their surnames, though it became fashionable for senior boys in responsible positions to have a Christian name tacked on. It seems heartless to call a little pig-tailed (are they still?) tot 'Metcalfe' or 'Hodgson'. Schoolgirls in the pages of Angela Brazil, and I think in life itself, usually sport both names, giving us such combinations as Prudence Willoughby, Blanche Merriweather or Dawn Westinghouse. A Christian name on its own will not do at all for, parents being conventional by nature, the school will no doubt end up

141

with eight Emmas and nine Susans and untold Sarahs.

Minor advantages are at once apparent, especially in the field of dramatic endeavour. No longer will reluctant young men of fifteen have to tog themselves up as Portia or Lady Macbeth, their chests suitably embellished for the occasion ('Please, sir, Henderson's lost one of his shapes').

To what extent can games become fully co-educational? Oundle has for many years been a distinguished rugger school, the scourge of the Midlands. But I somehow don't seem able to picture Dawn Westinghouse, sturdy as she may be, as school hooker (if you see what I mean), although the informality of the loose maul would certainly add a new and pleasing dimension to the game. Athletics appear to have more possibilities, in particular competitive running in which girls could compete on an equal footing and would indeed benefit from an in-built advantage in a close finish.

The future is indeed rosy and it is all very splendid, for when, long ago, I was a boy at Oundle, the only feminine influences allowed within a mile of us were the housemaster's wife, a remote and queenly presence who addressed each of us as 'darling', not always being fully assured of our names, and the matron, a wild Welsh lady called Miss Jones, whom one saw only when requiring clean socks or medicine or to have one's temperature taken in the vain hope of avoiding an OTC parade ('Oh, not you again, Marshall').

Such a strictly masculine ambience did not encourage the acquiring of many social graces and I was an outstandingly gauche teenager, unable to enter a room without sending tea-cups flying in all directions; hostesses rightly dreaded me. In today's friendlier and more human and relaxed conditions I might have blossomed. Perhaps Oundle could find a place for me. I still have my tuckbox somewhere.

THE BANNED PLAYED ON

As soon as I saw it stated somewhere or other that the Milky Way is made up of 100,000 million million stars I decided to stop worrying about the pound. It seemed rather petty. Let it go up or down or, if it feels like a change, sideways. I shan't mind.

Nor am I going to get agitated if my telly viewing is to be, shall we say, subject to scrutiny. This is, so to speak, where I came in for I first started writing lyrics and sketches for theatrical revues at a time when every single word uttered or sung had to be passed by the Lord Chamberlain.

In notes and memoranda his initials were used and he was referred to as the LC but, so sadly spinsterish and fussy was he that I always thought of him as Elsie.

Elsie used to get terribly worried about almost everything and in particular the work of that matchless revue writer, Herbert Farjeon. In one Farjeon sketch Hermione Baddeley was required to state that, as a confirmed and very cantankerous invalid, she found Bournemouth 'definitely constipating'.

Elsie didn't like that at all and a lively correspondence with the author began, the shocking word being eventually changed to 'costive', an adjective virtually unknown to the British public. However Miss Baddeley managed to make its meaning quite clear, banging out the word costive with such hearty relish that it became constipation in spades.

For reasons known only to herself, Elsie decided in 1925 to ban completely John van Druten's play, *Young Woodley*, a public school romance in which a house prefect falls in love with Laura, his housemaster's wife, an improbable, nay preposterous, happening in the school houses that I have known.

The trouble begins when Laura arrives in the prefects' study to complain about the juniors. 'It's the shrubbery,' she says in a memorable section of dialogue, 'the boys are using it' — as a short cut, I hasten to add, rather than for more static purposes requiring concealment. Drinking, for instance.

Perhaps what Elsie disliked was the fact that young Woodley wrote poetry (unhealthy stuff) and, when at tea and alone with Laura, spouted out a rather soupy sonnet of his own construction. Laura, overcome, permits an embrace, the stage directions reading: 'She buries her lips in his hair.' Disgusting, I do see.

But fair is fair and Elsie did have moments of sense and sweet reasonableness. A talented revue actor, Walter Crisham, wanted to do a number as a down-at-heels man in a grubby macintosh selling 'questionable photographic material', part of the lyric being: 'Buy my dirty postcards, they've all been smuggled through the coastguards.' Permission was, of course, instantly refused.

Later, however, the Lord Chamberlain, seeing the number performed on a private occasion, decided that it was done with such tact and charm and pathos and, unbelievably, taste, that he withdrew his objection. So hooray for that.

But then, alas, Elsie got up to her old tricks again, banning a harmless song about Queen Victoria, laying down the law about certain unacceptable gestures, and refusing to allow the statement from the stage that GOD is DOG spelt backwards. Beat that.

BBC GAGGED ME

Heartening news! The admirable but impoverished BBC is making substantial financial economies and I have direct evidence of this from Broadcasting House itself.

Wandering recently in its hinterland when recording a eulogy of the late, alas, Joyce Grenfell's delightful collection of nursery lore entitled *Nanny Says*, I was brought face to face with a door starkly labelled, in black paint, GENTS.

The word 'gentlemen' has nine letters while GENTS has but five and thus four lettersworth of paint had been saved, an example to all. What a pity that the word 'ladies' cannot be similarly shortened, the word LADS on a door merely causing confusion and red faces and cries of 'Pardon me!'

I first passed through the imposing BH doors in 1934 and before long I became involved in an incident the central matter of which might even today, and fifty-four years later, agitate the authorities, frequently harassed as they are by accusations of allowing indelicacies and promoting smut.

I used in those days to broadcast imitations of the enthralling schoolgirl stories of Miss Angela Brazil, and one of them that I proposed to give concerned a croquet tournament, the winner to receive a handsome croquet award sportingly donated by the Headmistress, Miss Pringle. To set the scene and give the full flavour of the tale, here are the closing sentences: 'To negotiate the last hoop, and peg smartly out, was for Gloria the work of a moment and cheer after cheer echoed round the ancient elms. She had won, she had won! Miss Pringle's prize balls were hers!'

145

The producer, as we then called him, got very fussed. 'But you can't possibly say that!' 'Why ever not?' I answered, the very picture, and rightly, of innocence. 'Well, it's . . . er . . . um . . . not very . . .' he muttered as he hunted for a word that would not reveal him to have a not totally untarnished mind. I let him flounder on and finally he said: 'I'm afraid you'll have to change it.'

The rehearsal was held up while we pondered the subject. I was determined to stick to my guns. 'Would it be better,' I suggested, 'if I said Miss Pringle's *championship* balls were hers?' He gave a startled shriek. 'Oh no, no, that's *much* worse.'

We thought again. I was helpfulness itself. 'Shall I say Miss Pringle's *case* of championship balls?' So dotty had the thing become that I was tempted to refer to 'a *slight* case of balls'.

'I can't settle this on my own,' he said at last. 'We'll have to push the whole thing up higher for a decision,' and off the file went to loftier regions for a ruling.

Time passed and meanwhile news reached us that the file was moving ever upwards, nobody caring to accept a responsibility that might land them in the soup.

Eventually, and I would add the word 'unbelievably' were not this entire episode true, our humble file landed on the desk of the Lord High Executioner, John Reith himself, who had practically invented broadcasting and was known to have puritanical views. A Scotsman, he was said to be something of a tyrant who had dealt ruthlessly with moral failings among his staff.

But he was also, it seemed, a realist and back his answer came. 'I see nothing wrong in this. Mr Marshall may certainly say what he has written. Ladies do not have, in any indelicate sense, the objects under discussion.'

So I went ahead. However, the BBC used then to have its own methods of punishing awkward customers and for a year or more I was but sparingly engaged.

THE CROQUET FINAL

'By Jimini, girls,' vociferated Madge Bellamy, leaping from bed and rattling back her cubie curtains. 'What a spifflicating day for the croquet final between Gloria Doubleday and Blodwen Parks. Come on, Gloria,' she carolled to her special chum, 'what about a tip-top sluice in the seniors' lavabo. How's your eye old girl, eh?'

'First rate thanks Madge,' riposted Gloria, rinsing herself vigorously with a copious spongeful of creamy suds. 'And I do hope Blodwen's in topping fettle, too,' she added, generously.

'Oh, Blodwen's still frowsting under her eiderdown,' scoffed Rosalie, 'she doesn't care a tinker's cuss for hygiene.'

'And another thing,' rydered Madge, 'it's common knowledge amongst the juniors that she keeps a bottle of Australian Burgundy in her boot-locker.' This was indeed true: poor Blodwen Parks had fallen a victim to the pleasures of the grape, and how she kept up the gruelling pace at croquet nobody could fathom.

By half past two that afternoon the atmosphere round Main Lawn had tensed almost to breaking-point. Blodwen, a triumphant sneer on her ashen face, was streets ahead, having coaxed her orange spheroid through hoop after hoop. Gloria bit her lip and bent low over her mallet. Her plaits flopped forward over her face but she tossed them relentlessly back, and in that grim gesture those watching sensed the Titanic struggle to come; Gloria meant to win, and it was as plain as a pikestaff. Her mallet rose, quivering like a thing possessed, then — *Bing*.

147

'Bravo, bravo,' chorused the juniors and, scarcely daring to open her eyes, Gloria realised from their cheers that she had roqueted Blodwen right out of position.

Gloria's blood was up and there was no holding her: it was *Bing* one minute, *Ping* the next.

Then, last hoop, and anybody's game.

Blodwen, with a daring fluke off Gloria's plimsole, had placed her coloured ovoid right in the mouth of the penultimate objective. Gloria steeled herself for a final effort: *Bang, Swoosh, Click*: — *Bang* — *Swoosh* — *Click*.

Then, something seemed to snap inside Blodwen, her mask dropped and she became a livid gibbering Thing. Forcing a dreadful oath from her lips she seized her heavy hickory mallet. 'Take that, you devil,' she hissed, and she hurled it at Gloria with the full force of her opulent biceps. Gloria leapt nimbly aside with all the agility of the trained athlete and the mallet, singing harmlessly past her, tinkled to rest against the Pankhurst railings.

To negotiate the last hoop, and peg smartly out, was for Gloria the work of a moment and cheer after cheer echoed round the ancient elms. She had won, she had won! Miss Pringle's (case of championship) balls was hers.

Later that evening there came a knock at her cubie. It was Blodwen.

'I say, Gloria,' she ventured, 'don't think me a softie but, well, I've come to eat humble pie. The best girl won this afternoon. Congratters, and shall we — shake?' Both girls fought back their tears for a space, then, when she could speak, 'Shake?' cried Gloria. 'I should jolly well think so. And I say, Blodwen, you've been looking a bit pasty lately. I've a ripe pippin in my locker. Kept it for morning but, may as well have it now. What do you say to our polishing it off, and keeping the doctor away, together?'

And the two girls snuggled cosily down, and munched and munched and munched.

NURSE DUGDALE
CALLING

(*A telephone rings*)

Hullo, this is the Phone-a-Psych Service, Instant Psychiatry By Telephone, Nurse Dugdale at the apparatus, can I help you?

You're a hotel telephone operator, and very nice too, dear. Now, what seems to be your trouble? Oh I see, on behalf of Room Eighty-two, well just put the person through, dear.

Hullo, this is the Phone-a-Psych Service. Good morning. Now before we start, just give me your name dear. Edie? And you're black? And you're in London? Splendid splendid. Now let me just get this right — you're a black girlie called Edie and you've got yourself into some sort of trouble. But Edie is a girlie's name dear, just fun talk for Edith. Over here, it means a girlie, dear. And you're a boysie. I see, and Edie dear there is no need to shout, nothing is to be gained by shouting and calm down dear because now I shall picture you as a black boysie instead of as a black girlie.

Well now, dear, what is your problem? Speak quite frankly, dear, we are discretion itself. Oh I see. Well, it is true that the lady you mention does live in London, but she's also partly in Berkshire and partly in Scotland and partly in Norfolk. Now here, now there, dear, and of course sometimes abroad. No dear, we all like her very much but we do not go and call on her unless invited to do so, and, Edie dear, I'm finding it very difficult to hear what you're saying because in the background there's a sort of clanking sound of something metallic. It's your medals. Of course. And you're in pyjams. Quite so.

Well, just lay them down somewhere where they can't clank, dear, and then we can lower our voices.

What? Oh you *are* in a muddle, dear! The lady is already married! She has been married for many happy years and she has four children. No dear, I really don't think that she would like to join up with other ladies and form part of some sort of 'group', chummy and friendly though it would all doubtless be. Edie dear, you're shouting again, and somewhere back there when you were speaking I thought I caught a funny word which I do *not* understand and which I never want to hear from you again. Edie, you're shouting. Edie, STOP IT. Oh operator, operator, can you hear me, op — oh there you are. Tell the hotel desk dear to rush some sedatives up to Room Eighty-two. I'm afraid Edie's got herself a tiny bit upset.

DIY

Quite a long time ago, I bought a new motor car, Goodwood Green in colour and sprouting every known dashboard accessory. At the time, it was the best car that I could afford. I've never been one of those who willingly changes cars. I feel a sort of loyalty towards them and we tend to stay married until the very end. I have this particular car still. We've been together now for thirteen years and it really don't seem a day too much. It has been the kindest of friends: patient, quiet and ready to help. It has lived outside in all weathers for the whole of its life and it's never once complained or failed to start. I haven't, of course, the very faintest idea what makes it go. I know, naturally, that you put petrol in but after that I am lost and the mists mercifully close.

But the other day, in the car's front pocket and underneath the packets of boiled sweets, I came upon a brochure called *Owner's Handbook*, still exactly in the place where the supplier put it all those years ago, still in its cellophane see-through envelope. I got it out and turned the pages and I'm extremely glad that for thirteen years I haven't known what's been going on under the bonnet. Life would have been a *nightmare* of worry. What of my valve clearances? What, and indeed where, is my throttle linkage? Is my fuel pump sediment bowl chock-a-block with sediment? Is my carburettor float chamber floating as it should? Above all, is it time to flush out my crankcase?

I've heard keen motorists sometimes speak knowledgeably of gaskets and so I feel that I've 'done', so to speak, gaskets, but what of these other things, some of which sound so human? Clutch friction area, for example, starter air passage, sump capacity, initial advance to the crankshaft, telescopic shock absorbers, downdraughts and impeller-assisted circulation and valve bleed and circulatory balls.

Well, I've put the brochure right back where it came from and I'm trying, like others who have had unfortunate experiences, to 'forget'.

GOING IT ALONE

Despite the fact that in my happy schooldays at Oundle, that supremely practical school, every encouragement and facility was present for doing effective work in both wood and metal, that particular educational seed fell, in my case, on the most barren of grounds. Not caring much for oil, let alone whirring lathes, I wore gloves in the metal workshops, greatly upsetting the instructors, and now, hopeless with my hands, I cannot knock a nail into a wall in order to hang up a tasteful coloured reproduction without the plaster instantly disintegrating and depositing 'Rogue Elephant Charging' in smithereens at my feet. On a humbler level, I cannot even open one of those delightful padded postal book bags (*Pull Tab Sideways*) without getting covered in a grey snowstorm of powdered paper pulp.

But now, inspired by the splendid, if noisy, example of that enthusiastic Yorkshire resident who, my newspaper tells me, worked so vigorously at embellishing his house that he allegedly 'vibrated' into the other side of his semi-detached, the other side subsequently propelling, by way of a polite hint to shut up, a brick at his double-glazing, I am myself going into the DIY world in rather a big way. I am not semi but fully detached and so I can vibrate away like anything but I plan, as it happens, to begin in quite a quiet and modest manner.

I've purchased heaps of Do-It-Yourself magazines and I'm going to kick off by cleaning my corroded ballvalve. I merely have to remove, it says, my split pin and rub my body flanges with emery paper and thus restore my flushing to all its former power. Oh well, all right. Then I shall move smoothly to my carpentry bench and construct from elm (there is, alas, lots about) a 'natural look cheeseboard', just asking myself what on earth an unnatural cheeseboard would look like. After that, and with Christmas so near, I'm going to check over my festoon of fairy lights. If they reveal a malfunction, it means, they tell me, an electrical fault in my festoon.

Happy contentment is everywhere, and merry jokes too (an advertisement for a fan with which to freshen 'the smallest room' talks of the fan being able to bring 'an air to the throne'). The illustrations reveal jolly faces on all sides and none jollier than those grouped cheerily round an enterprising chap who has managed ('More sherry, anybody?') to turn an old chest of drawers into a drinks bar. Somewhere perhaps, booze being the price it is, there are instructions for turning an old drinks bar into a chest of drawers.

And then, having laid my 'blush pink' tiling in my luxi-kitchen-cum-dinette and erected a shower cabinet with a multi-spray adjustable nozzle in the bathroom, splash curtains everywhere, I'm going to alter all the lighting. Away with those dusty old lamps, it suggests, and 'pick out special features in your home' with spotlights. The bother here is that I'm a bit short on special features. There are no mysterious alcoves, no spiral staircases (and it tells you how to make *them*). My gum-boots would, I suppose, hardly rank as being in any way special. Would, I wonder, my dear old Cousin Madge, a regular visitor, qualify as a feature and submit to being spotlit? Time will tell.

And later on I must tackle the whole problem of 'louvre doors'. I'm far from clear what they are for. They seem to be on the principle of a sort of petrified Venetian blind, and they appear in cupboards. But why? I shall just regard them as being, for the time being, beyond me and try not to notice ('*No* louvres, my dear!') my friends' horrified looks.

I see that I am not the only D I Y worker with worries. The correspondence columns bristle with anxieties. Can one apply weed-killer to a moss-covered bungalow roof? What's to be done for the best if sap exudes from a brand new patio door? And who can recommend 'a good washable grout' for use between ceramic tiles on the top of a 'breakfast bar'?

Now, what on earth can a breakfast bar be? I don't at all want to be left out of things, and any moment now I shall be able to emerge, purple and breathing heavily, from my very own personalised sauna, that modish status symbol. But a bar for breakfast? Do I have to perch up on a stool at it, tucking into my Krunchykorn and wolfing that weird-sounding comestible, 'battered cod-pieces' which, in the reign of Elizabeth I, would have conjured up such a very painful picture? Why can't I have my breakfast at a table just like anybody else? And somewhere in the mags there's a table laid for six that turns in a twinkling, and you'll hardly credit it, into a double bed. That would, in every sense, suit me down to the ground.

WITHIN MY POWERS

For once I find myself, normally one of nature's slowcoaches, ahead of somebody else in the race of life and in this case ahead of no less a surprising person than President Carter himself. Serious readers of this column cannot fail to recall that several weeks ago I drew attention to what will undoubtedly be posterity's reproachful attitude to our drunken squandering of those precious and irreplaceable liquids, petrol and oil (perhaps they are basically the same thing. I've never quite understood). And then, up recently spoke the President, just echoing my very own words. I also, on *Any Questions?*, begged our Prime Minister, then Mr Callaghan, to be a man, appear on the box and urge us all to save fuel and to drive about less. For the average person, two car journeys in five are totally unnecessary. Did he take any notice? No he did not. Placid and rosily self-confident as ever, all he did was to announce that we in this country are on the verge of 'a golden decade', upon which intimation of impending disaster and catastrophe, countless people had heart attacks and I looked out and dusted down my passport and pestered travel agents for cheap one-way trips to Tristan da Cunha. I'm far from sure where it is but it sounds splendidly distant, and that first name gives it a delightfully musical and romantic ring.

But alas, although it is certainly in my nature to desert any sinking ship on which I happen to find myself and scramble to dry land as quickly as possible, I'm now too old to go scuttling off from England and so I'm nobly going to make shift as best I can to lead the way in our little community and pioneer, as the

President suggests (such an example to our chap), attempts at additional sources of power. I am not so bold and vain as to imagine that I can do this on my own but a book, American in origin, has come my way, edited by Carol Hupping Stoner, and it is called *Producing Your Own Power* and it is a perfect mine of information. Clever Ms Carol Hupping Stoner has gathered together experts on various power-providers that, when the petrol gives out (sooner than one imagines, it seems, and I gather that the final completion of our M roads is timed to coincide exactly with our empty tanks), are going to make just all the difference and are, what is more, in inexhaustible supply. I refer, of course, to wind, sun, water, gravity, wood and cow-pats.

All of these are fully obtainable in Devon and so let us start with the easiest, which is the last named, and by it we are naturally to understand dung in all its forms. Carol Hupping Stoner's nominees here are the happy couple, Sharon and James Whitehurst, and they set the ball rolling with an arresting section called 'Our Four-Cow Bio-Gas Plant', for we are, as you see, concerned with the production of another variety of natural gas, methane. Methane is, of course, our dear old friend, marsh-gas, and to construct it you will need a Methane Gas Digester, and into the Digester you put anything that's going in the way of what I've already mentioned. I'm sorry to say that the actual inside of a Digester isn't all that attractive. Reading the layers from the top down, they go bio-gas, scum, digested sludge, spent slurry and, if you're doing it in a pond out of doors, all these items rest on a bed of what is unfortunately called pea gravel. Through this mixture, large gas bubbles rise slowly and sullenly to the surface and go, presumably, pop! From time to time, you should seize a prong and 'agitate' what I said before. For further reading, dip into back numbers of the *Sewage Works Journal*, the fountain-head of all that is best in this useful sphere.

The Whitehursts don't miss a trick. 'The size of your live-stock has a lot to do with the amount of manure produced.'

Nor is this all. They fire the imagination by stating that a man called Harold Bates managed to build a car that was powered solely by chicken manure. Indeed, this substance appears to be, in its field, the most prized of all and our authors, though they do tend to run on a little about its virtues, are liberal in their praise of it and of chickens in general. So it is with this that we had better start, but how? 'Myrtlebank', which, once polluted with ducks and Wyandottes, now boasts no livestock. My Cousin Madge's geese are long since disappeared. The prudent local wartime custom of keeping a few hens died out some time ago. However, I rather fancy that somewhere in the hinterland of the Bultitudes' extensive premises, there are some chickens, probably a rather fancy breed. These helpful feathered bipeds are never mentioned, for we naturally have loftier subjects to discuss, but I recollect that when the wind has been in the right direction, I have heard contended cluckings. I will wait until they (the Bultitudes) are once more in Cannes ('How can you *bear* not to go at least twice a year?') and then nip round and have a look. And what's more, I'll take a bucket with me.

For the wind section and electric generators, Carol Hupping Stoner puts us into the capable hands of Henry Clews, who refers to all houses as homesteads, who prepares 'handy-dandy' little wind tables, who has his thoughtful moments ('About the only thing you can say for certain concerning wind is that it is always changing') and who wants each of us to erect in our gardens a forty-foot high steel tower with on the top of it one of Quirk's 'Brushless Windplants' (change gearbox oil once every five years) and make our very own electricity. Don't be too ambitious. A twelve-foot diameter propeller is quite OK for starters and it should revolve at a mere 150 revolutions per minute. The bigger the slower, of course, and the huge 175-foot propeller on an eminence called, apparently, Grandpa's Knob in Vermont, revolves at only twenty-eight rpm. Get going immediately.

But I see that I've left all too little space to tell you what I plan additionally and energywise in the way of undershot water wheels, simple pile drivers, hydraulic rams complete with clack valves and snifter holes, not to speak of sections of wire gauze to prevent frogs getting sucked in with the water and forming part of the mechanism. And, in connection with power from water, 'If you have not had welding experience,' says our adviser, 'you may have to buy your own turbine.' Quite so. I've long since settled for that. And among Carol Hupping Stoner's further treats are a Mr Kern (not, unfortunately, Jerome), who is in charge of wood and who tells us all there is to know about Count Rumford and his comprehensive essay, 'Count Rumford on Chimney Fireplaces,' which startled the world in 1800 and is as viable today as ever it was.

If you're planning to look me up in Appleton, you can find your way to it by watching out for a forest of steel towers, the sounds of whirring turbines, the mad cackling of poultry, the clonks of the pile drivers and the clacks of the clack valves, and the fragrances from the Digesters. And if you decide to press on to Moretonhampstead, I shall quite understand.

MAKING DO

Readers, no slouches when it comes to writing letters, were agreeably quick to show their kind appreciation of an article I recently provided, now that electricity charges soar ever upwards, on the subject of alternative sources of power, extolling the virtues of such homely things as cow-pats and wind, not necessarily together. There was, it is true, a correspondent with a Knightsbridge address who wrote regretfully to say that, hunt about as she may, cow-pats in the neighbourhood of Harrods seemed to be few and far between. I of course answered at once, reminding her that the justifiably proud telegraphic address of that unrivalled emporium used to be, if memory serves, EVERYTHING, LONDON. She has merely to step inside and head smartly for the Information Desk.

I am happily now in a position to follow up my helpful words on wind-machines and marsh gas and share with you the many good things to be found in two illustrated glossy-backs that have come my way, *Survival Scrapbook I* (*shelter*) and *Survival Scrapbook 2* (*food*). The compiler is the splendid Stefan Szczelkum, to whom, for obvious and euphonious reasons, I will henceforward refer to as Mr S. Survival from what is not made very clear, nor do we know whether the big bang has gone off, but I think we may assume that all buildings have been flattened, gas and electricity are a thing of the past, the baker calls no more, the doors of the Co-op are closed, and we are all managing as best we can on our own home ground and on our own, a real challenge to us here in our remote part of

162

Devon where the average age of the doughty inhabitants is around the seventy mark.

One excitedly turns Mr S's packed pages and instantly the eye is caught and held by a purply-tinted photograph showing a 'dobo' or tree-house for unmarried women in Melanesia. This is clearly the absolutely ideal refuge, apart from a rickety bamboo ladder thirty-feet high, for my unmarried Cousin Madge, now a very game eighty-six. She is not Melanesian, but the text indicates that this little hurdle can be surmounted. One of the vital things appears to be choice of tree ('Be sure it is the tree you want to live with'). After Mr S. has examined and discarded the possibilities of a vast bird's nest made of dried mud (not, I trust, saliva-bound as with some of our feathered friends), we find Madge installed, after testing the branches by swinging on them, high up in an oak and on a roomy wooden platform thatched with fragrant heather culled from the spacious grounds of 'Myrtlebank'. Thoughtful people, realising the hardship for an octogenarian of periodic and perilous ascents and descents from a tree-house, will now be tactfully wondering how Madge is going to 'manage'. Calm yourselves, for this problem has been already foreseen and we have hoisted up with her a 'Porta Pott', which is what its name implies. Madge has only to lower the contraption from time to time on the rope which she has herself plaited from river-gathered rushes and all's to rights again.

Meanwhile here at ground level all is bustle and activity. Of what is luncheon in the tree-house going to consist? Even by Shanks's pony, it is the merest step to Teignmouth where fish abound and could be netted, though here Mr S. sounds a mysterious and warning note. 'Beware,' he counsels, 'of fish with flabby skin, slimy gills, box-shaped bodies and deep-set eyes.' Nor are deep-set eyes all. 'The food value of fish meat varies with its physiological state, the most important factor of which is the sexual state of the fish.' Here's a poser! How can one tell? Obliging as MacFisheries' assistants invariably are, one can hardly point to a haddock lying, the picture of innocence, on the slab, lower the voice and lean forward with an embarrassed 'Er, excuse me but . . .'

So for safety's sake we'll forego fish and settle for something less agitating and here Mr S. provides a total bafflement and diversion in the shape of Yin and Yang, neither of them of much practical value to an elderly person perched in a tree. Bang in the middle of the food section, we are told that 'Yin and Yang are the two aims of infinity, absolute oneness, God or the infinite pure expansion.' Then it's back to tuck again, only to find that food has been divided into Yin or Yang. The Yin First XI contains asparagus, mushrooms, yoghurt, wine and bananas, the Yang players countering strongly with carrots, eggs, goat's milk, apples and pheasants. Hopeless to shout up details of Yin and Yang to Madge and ask her to choose, so we just send up a balanced and fully edible meal of *les crudités* (bladder campion, fireweed and marsh wound-wort), plankton spread on dawn-baked slices of acorn bread, Chef's Choice *mousse de* grasshopper, seaweed salad, with frogs on horseback as a savoury. Not long after, down whizzes the Porta Pott.

Wherever you look, and with no further references to infinite pure expansion, Mr S provides a handy survival wrinkle. Always take your boots into the sleeping-bag with you. Serious frostbite may be alleviated by placing the affected feet into 'a warm recess of your own, or someone else's armpit or crutch'. A coat fashioned from Chinese rice-straw makes an AI mac. When sleeping in the open, avoid rheumatics by choosing a place where cows are known to sleep. If your luck is in, you'll be over a concealed spring which 'generates beneficial spiral forces', and, if your luck is really in, the cows won't have lingered long. Remember that wigwams sixty-foot long *must* have three-inner uprights. Why not make your very own Wendy house out of laminated newspaper soaked in wallpaper paste? Wild boars can get enticed into snares by the sound of the flute (they are especially susceptible to seventeenth-century composers). If you pretend not to see adult rabbits and just saunter along, humming a tune, a sudden grab may be successful.

If you're both peckish and penniless, don't forget that blood donors get free tea and biscuits.

DON'T JUST SIT THERE

It is not often, plodding modestly along as one does on Life's Treadmill and never saying boo to a goose (rather an unproductive activity, don't you find?), that one considers oneself to have been humiliated by, of all things, a gardening tip, but such has recently been my sad portion.

Normally, gardening periodicals ('Prick out your lobelias') provide instructions ('Mulch your perennials') that are more or less ('Now's the time to graft your cacti') within my limited range and so, and only the other day, I turned eagerly to a revered gardening magazine to see with what delightful task I should be busying myself. The Hint of the Week was quite a short one. It just said: 'Continue to cut your asparagus.'

'Continue', if you please. This seems to imply that the ordinary person, and all over the country, has now being going snip-snip for weeks, rising at dawn to harvest the succulent shoots from an asparagus bed half a mile long where the thing grows like a weed.

I only wish that I had been so snipping. I greatly enjoy asparagus and, with buttery fingers, can slobber and dribble with the best despite the austere vegetable's reproachful reminders, later in the day, that one has been eating it. And there is the happy childhood classroom howler to relish: 'Jesus Christ was betrayed by Judas Asparagus.'

I did once own a sort of asparagus bed and, on being informed by a long-ago Hint of the Week that asparagus welcomed seaweed as a nourishing enrichment, I hurried off to Teignmouth and, thrusting firmly aside kiddies with

166

buckets, scooped up a generous armful of the fragrant marine algae and, hastening home, I spread it tenderly all over the bed. The asparagus instantly died. A mocking friend told me that it was obvious that the asparagus was sulking because the seaweed hadn't come from Torquay, which it plainly considered to be a rather more chic seaside resort.

Never mind. I've cheered up no end because I am just back from a jolly month's holiday in Jamaica and New York and if you are good enough to notice a fresh vigour in my prose, an increased variety in my thought patterns and, in general, an altogether more rounded personality, let me say at once that I owe the whole caboosh, if there is such a word, to American Airlines.

Settling myself in my seat for the flight from Montego Bay to Kennedy Airport and reassuring myself as to the underseat presence of my life jacket (making a mental note to, should it be necessary, hold my nose during splashdown), I found in that sort of rack thing on the back of the seat in front, a brochure entitled *Exercises for Relaxed Travel*. The brochure's general theme was: 'Don't just sit there!'

The exercises, I was told, could be accomplished with seat belt safely fastened and would relax my muscles and stimulate my circulation. I got busy at once. Exercise Number One was not difficult: 'Lean head forward as far as possible,' a negligible distance in my case, and then: 'Lean head to the side,' first this way, then that. Lulled by the apparent ease and simplicity of the thing, I embarked on Exercise Number Two and was at once in deep trouble: 'Let head drop back, jaw relaxed, and look up at the overhead compartment of the row behind you. Arch upper back. Feel stretch under your chin.' Here I had a choice, being the lucky possessor of more than one.

Quite soon the pace hotted tremendously up: 'Hug yourself . . . move rib cage to front . . . make a circle with one shoulder at a time . . . reach up toward the air vent . . . lean over to the floor as if to pick up something you've dropped . . .

turn your upper body to the right and look behind you.'

By now the lady on my left, pince-nezed, middle-aged and American, was looking startled, and worse was to come: 'Pick one foot up off the floor . . . raise your whole leg . . . make circles in the air with the raised foot . . . circle eight times to the right and eight times to the left.'

I left it there, having spotted, and just in time, a warning notice: 'The service of liquor is forbidden to any passenger who appears to be intoxicated.'

TRAVEL TALK

I have a wild passion for hotels, *all* hotels whether good, bad or awful. The dusty potted palm in the hallway, the busty proprietress in the rather grubby sateen blouse bravely beaming a welcome, the fusty, musty smells, the difficulty ('I'll just ring for Jim') of getting luggage taken upstairs — all is fascination and so in my three weeks of luxi-travel I aim to cram in as many old friends as possible.

I have, in fact, been very lucky. London, for instance. Driving there from Cambridge in an Austin Seven in the 1920s, I dared not venture further into the capital than the imposing Russell Hotel (thirteen shillings and sixpence bed and breakfast, and a four-courser at that) and there I happily stayed, on and off, for years. So, one night there, followed by the Ritz, the Savoy and Claridges where, in wartime and in relatively empty London, one could stay without going bankrupt.

Then off, jet-propelled, to Monte Carlo and the Hotel de Paris, so handy for the Casino — not that it greatly matters to me where my hotels are. As I never move out of them, it can be Tahiti or Reading for all I care.

Then away again, by Concorde, to New York and the Algonquin, with its splendidly hung-over aura of Dorothy Parker. And then back again to such home delights as Taunton's County Hotel and Marlborough's Ailesbury Arms.

I shan't, I think, break new ground and go to Russia. A

friend recently there spoke of poor service, glum faces and an absence of vodka. Indeed, there was only one crumb of pleasure in his vast Moscow hotel. This was his room number. It was 1812.

FUNNY FACE

One must clutch at life's meagre solaces as and when they chance to come along and I am extremely glad not to have to gaze more often than is absolutely necessary for washing it, shaving it or brushing its hair, at my face. Catching sight of it sometimes by mistake in an unexpected reflection in a shop window, I gasp and start back in horror. Can this be, I ask myself, the pencil-slim undergraduate who arrived at Cambridge in 1928 with the whole world before him and determined to do as little work as possible? Yes it can. My face is now like one of those large round loaves constructed at home by panicky housewives during a bread shortage — rather a lot of it, with odd bulges here and there and all of it pretty dull. But at least the alarmingly spacious visual area has not been increased by baldness. My hair, if now white, is still all there, though said by mocking and envious friends to be actually a wig from the famous theatrical *perruquier*, Gustave.

This distinguished name reminds me of Lilian Baylis and one of her Old Vic actresses. Striding into the actress's dressing-room after a first performance, Miss Baylis said briskly: 'That wig must go back to Gustave.' The actress, appalled, stammered out: 'But Miss Baylis, this isn't a wig, it's my own hair.' 'I don't care whose it is,' Miss Baylis replied, 'it must go back to Gustave.'

Twenty years ago my face, looming large even then, was at risk. I was in New York and staying at the delightful Algonquin Hotel, celebrated for its wits' Round Table (and how fearfully agitating lunch at it must have been amid so

173

many rather self-conscious funninesses). No hotel welcomes more warmly eccentrics under its wing. A lady, resident there and well known to me for many years, chose to do action-painting in her sitting-room and greatly enjoyed flicking blobs of colour about. In course of time she had managed to action-paint the room's carpet, walls and furniture, together with every exposed surface in her bedroom. For all I know she liberally action-painted the room service personnel when they arrived with meals. The splendid hotel authorities had taken these vigorous artistic endeavours firmly on the chin.

The lady had many black friends in the world of jazz music, in which she was rightly held in high esteem. One of them, calling on her at dusk one day and wearing a bright blue suit, mistook her door and entered another room. With his face and hands merging invisibly into the corridor's darkness, it looked to anybody short-sighted as though a bright blue suit was walking by itself, unaided and uninvited, into the apartment. Loud screams and great confusions from the ancient female occupant.

Among the hotel's other eccentrics was a tallish lady with a curled lip and a forbidding look. Though doubtless a dear at heart, she was one of those people who, without realising it, speak their thoughts aloud and I was warned to avoid her if possible. She seemed to haunt the lifts and formed a daily hazard. I first heard her in action when some wretched woman, just in from shopping in New York's icy and snowy (it was January) streets and on her way up to her room, found herself suddenly addressed and speeded happily on by this female menace with the words: 'You have very coarse skin.' My turn was to come. Descending alone from my room and on my way to shop in Bloomingdales (a vast and tip-top amalgam of Liberty's and Waring & Gillow and the Army & Navy Stores), the lift stopped at a floor en route to the ground and in she stepped. Down we went, while she stared unwaveringly at me. Silence. I thought I had escaped, but no. Just two words. 'Pudding face.' Well, it could have been a lot worse.

To me, New York City, however knee-deep in litter and muggers it may be said to be, remains a magical place and I keep abreast of all that is brightest and best on the American scene via the pages of the *New Yorker*. The London club of which I am so contentedly a part sells off at an advantageously cut rate, after a decent pause to allow the widest possible readership in the club rooms, back numbers of its magazines and I was lucky enough to scoop the ownership of this matchless feast of wit and enjoyment and good writing and information. Taking my spoils home, I can read at leisure of the sort of activities my American friends are indulging in, baffling though some of these may currently be (can it really now be possible to reach for the telephone and 'dial-a-joke' and how long will it be before this frightful amenity reaches us here?). For example, I see advertised a 'Harpsichord kit'. I take this to mean basic materials and blueprints with which to fashion in the home your very own personalised harpsichord and containing, I expect, the kind of mysterious instructions that for ever rule me out of the home harpsichord market. ('Slide walnut swivel-bar A-G into slotted cherrywood groove L-T, trim off nodules, assemble and adjust keyboard mechanism and then away you go on a joyous fragment from Scarlatti.')

Well then, available for both sexes in polished brass or copper and giving a 'constant boost to his or her confidence' comes the 'ego bracelet' featuring upon it the bold statement for all to see, 'DAMN I'M GOOD'. Again, how long before these contraptions reach our shores? Bracelets of any sort are not much worn in Appleton and such an eye-catching adornment would cause raised eyebrows over the rectory tea-cups, the rector probably not realising that 'good' here stands for 'efficient and successful' and is quite without any moral significance. Coupled as it is with the word 'Damn', the generally boastful effect would be unfortunate in the extreme. Consternation in the village would be complete were I to be seen in one of the T-shirts that seem to be all the rage over there and which have a wide variety of human faces printed on them. Who's afraid of Virginia Woolf? Well, I am for a start (and sick to death of her too) but here she is, visually available and gloomily pensive on a T-shirt. I could also appear, 'handsomely and washably screened on quality 100% cotton', as Bach, Amelia Earhart, Freud, Plato, Edgar Allan Poe, Pavlova and Gertrude Stein, none of them names or faces with which our village is entirely familiar ('Excuse me, is that Mrs Thatcher?').

There is another American availability that has always completely flummoxed me. I refer to 'sweat shirts'. Are these shirts to put on after violent exercise, or a kind of Turkish bath adjunct to help induce healthful sweat? Do interviewees wear them to help mop up nervous and unwelcome perspirations? My bewilderment is made complete by an advertisement photograph showing a pretty lady as fresh as a daisy in an 'ankle-length hooded sweatshirt'. It includes 'neck-to-navel zipper front, a hood for an air of mystery, and a roomy pouch-pocket', and one is encouraged to look on it not only as 'the good old slouch-around Saturday morning sweatshirt' but as a possibility for Saturday night as well and, even, boudoir time.

So many puzzlements there are. Do they really manage to sell 'Magnetic Soap Hangers' (press metal into your soap and then click the fragrant tablet to the wall)? Who positively uses a Vertical Car Compass ('Get headed in the right direction')? Can there actually be in Tennessee a town with the worrying name of Lynchburg? There is only one way to find out. I must go over again and see.

TRAVELLING HOPEFULLY

Partly because of my advanced years and the necessity to keep as calm as possible (blood pressure, and all that) and partly because I am keen on taking the fullest advantage of all the mini-benefits so sparingly dished out to us Senior Citizens, I now always travel first class, and therefore relatively uncrumpled, on our high speed, inner-city railways. Though the attack launched by courageous Corelli Barnett in *The Times* on the new-fashioned, open-plan cattle trucks dreamt up by the finest minds in British Rail was fully justified (vilely hard seats, odious colour schemes, the impossibility of anywhere propping the head and resting it comfortably for sleeping purposes, and the questionably delicious food that only expense accounts can afford), in the first class there is undoubtedly slightly more space and the percentage of 'kiddies' running disturbingly to and fro is smaller. By the way, an umbrella deftly thrust sideways out into the gangway can occasionally trip one of them up, bring it down and thus provide a valuable discouragement. Feign anxious solicitude when mothers look suspiciously at you. Parental control of children has now become as ineffective here as it has always been in America, so let us all do what we can.

Travelling recently from Exeter to London, the train stopped, as so often, at Reading, presumably to scoop up from fairly nearby Heathrow those air travellers who had now decided to press on by rail. Apart from being the fountain-head of tasty biscuits, and its interesting literary associations with Oscar Wilde (so difficult in youth to discover what exactly he had *done*, innocent questions merely producing lowered voices and 'Sh, dear!'), Reading is not perhaps the most fascinating of towns, though in this respect I must be careful what I say by way of disparagement. Chatting recently with an old chum, the delightful Jean Metcalfe, on the BBC's almost dementedly jolly and joky-voiced morning Open House programme, I drew attention at one point to what I considered to be the non-pleasures of Hull, and within three minutes an outraged resident had telephoned, and at peak cost time too, demanding an apology (instantly provided). I have now learnt my lesson. During our pause at picturesque and memory-haunted Reading, two elderly and nondescript ladies, clutching air-bags and duty-free substances, made as though to enter our coach, drawing back politely when they saw that it was not the class for which they had tickets. Upon which, a ticket-collector suddenly appeared, encouraged them in and settled them down, announcing in ringing tones and giving us all a firm look: 'This coach has now been down-graded.' Your sense of shock will be as great as mine. Was there ever such an insult and smack in the eye? When I purchased my expensive first-class seat at St David's Station, Exeter, where all is invariably courtesy and charm, nobody thought to warn me that I was going to be ignominiously and brutally down-graded at colourful, leafy and amenity-packed Reading. If I was the fuming kind, with a really spectacular thrombosis just round the corner, I would have fumed all the way to Paddington.

My father used, pre-War, to fume freely. By no means everything on the, to me, faultless Great Western was to his liking. He was apt sometimes to ask train-drivers at journey's end why they had had to drive their engines 'so jerkily'. The replies were lost in escaping steam. Just as well. Another of his mild eccentricities was, when we went away on holiday and the house was shut up, to close and lock the piano, removing the key. This always seemed to me to be hard luck on burglars who, after they had stuffed our silver and my mother's Persian lamb coat into a large bag labelled 'SWAG', might want tunefully to celebrate their haul with a few Chopin *études* or, in more thoughtful and grateful vein, a keyboard setting of *Bless This House*.

We lived then at Newbury and I noticed no such train imperfections for the railway-line ended in London, and in London there were theatres, however jerkily we might reach them. It was possible, a fact which becomes increasingly hard to believe, in those days to 'do' a matinée, as racy people phrased it, at a cost of slightly less than one pound, a sum known, again only to the racy, as a Bradbury or 'Brad' ('I say, old bean, lend me a Brad'), after the Bank of England official who signed the note and promised the bearer to shell out, on demand, twenty shillings. The lopped-off monosyllable reminds me happily of a winning entry in a long-ago *New Statesman* Competition for monosyllabic advertisements: 'Prog. coup. wish meet prog. coup. view share hol. bung. Sex ab. no ob.' We must, I fancy, assume that the 'ab.' is a shortened form of either 'aberrations' or 'abnormalities'. 'Ob.' is, of course, 'objection'.

But to our pound's worth, and the year (around 1926). The return railway fare to Paddington (crumpled travel) was six shillings and ninepence. The cost of the bus to Piccadilly was negligible (three pence, I suppose, if that). The four-course lunch on the first floor gallery of the Café Royal (and what a rip one felt!) came to three shillings and sixpence (waiter delighted, apparently, with sixpence). An upper circle seat for whatever Binnie Hale or Cicely Court-neidge or Gertrude Lawrence happened to be in at the time was five shillings, programme sixpence. Even with a reckless order of tea in the interval, you were about two bob in hand on your return home, ears still a-tingle with melody for those were, indeed, the days when, emerging from any popular musical entertainment by Gershwin or Coward or Richard Rodgers, there were in your head at least three tunes that refused for weeks to dislodge themselves. And in addition to the joy of seeing again one's favourite performers, there was

179

an astonishing range of available matinées. Every play had two a week and some — *The Ghost Train, Sunny, The Farmer's Wife* — had three.

On my return from one of these matinée jaunts (I think it must have been *Oh Kay*, which combined Gershwin and Miss Lawrence), a piece of unexpected good fortune came my way. I was seated alone in a compartment of the six pm out of Paddington and we were barely rattling through Ealing when there entered from the corridor somebody of about my own age (seventeen), followed shortly after by two older men of a *louche*-looking, race-going type. Suspicious. As we went whizzing through Slough, they invited the younger one to play, at a Bradbury a time, what I think is called Spot The Lady or The Three Card Trick — the identification of the back of the Queen of Spades from two other cards juggled swiftly about. In next to no time the young man had won quite a tidy sum. The performance was, of course, being set up for my benefit. The three of them were in league. I suppose that I looked, sitting there in my tidy, grey pin-stripe theatre-going suit, affluent and fully fleeceable. Soon they turned to me. Would I care to have a go? 'Yes,' I said, greatly daring in view of my remaining two shillings but knowing that they always encouraged victims with an early win. The cards shot about and I picked out without difficulty the queen and was handed a pound note. 'Here we go again,' they said. 'Thank you, no,' I primly replied, 'I have played sufficiently.' Amazement, disbelief, realisation, anger, fury, and those looks that are called 'ugly' and promise fisticuffs. I was contemplating tugging the communication cord (five pounds for Improper Use, and what use could be more proper than mine?) when the guard happened to pass along the corridor and I nipped quickly out and engaged him in animated conversation, subsequently locking myself in the lavatory until we reached Newbury.

Fairly disreputable behaviour all around, really, but it meant a free matinée the next week (*The Last of Mrs Cheyney*, if memory serves and worth every penny of the serious risk to life and limb).

ON THE ROAD

Not very much that could be called agreeable has been happening to us recently but if you chance to own and use a car, prepare yourselves for outstandingly heartening tidings (I am not referring to anything so mundane as a possible reduction in petrol charges for we are here dealing with matters altogether loftier and of the spirit).

Even those motorists among us whose memories awheel go back, like mine, to the pioneering days of starting-handles and goggles and dangerous dickey seats ('Where's your aunt gone?') nevertheless share in a generous bouquet handed out to us Men of the Tarmac by none other than the Transport Under-Secretary in person.

After my fifty years of blameless conduct at the steering-wheel, gamely tooting my way round sharp corners and renowned for the fluid grace of my hand signals (my 'I am about to turn left' has been especially admired), it is extremely cheering to be informed by this official of, presumably, Transport House, that 'British drivers are among the best-behaved and safest in the world'.

There now! What a delightful outpouring of praise to treasure and I do not wish to detract from this glowing testimonial when I say that I simply cannot imagine from which happy kerbside, adoration in his face and eyes misting over with the wonder of it all, the Under-Secretary has been observing these well-behaved British drivers going so safely about their business.

It was not always so. My early motoring experiences

involved being a passenger of my mother, for whom the open road was far from being her natural element. Though unselfish in every other way, she certainly insisted on her share of the highway and therefore drove firmly on the crown, with a hint of right in it. To get past her from behind was not easy ('Why is that wretched man honking at me?') and to pass her when going in the opposite direction had its problems and in my childhood I fell to wondering why cars approaching us seemed always to be half in the ditch and full of scowling faces.

My mother did not exactly move in motoring circles but she had a friend called Sylvia who also drove and who, puzzled that her presence in a built-up area always created such despondency and alarm, with children screaming and shoppers scurrying for cover, discovered some years later that her assumption that the thirty mph sign meant that you had to drive at thirty mph precisely and not a single mph less, was incorrect.

And it was Sylvia who, proceeding at a lively pace down a country lane in rural Berkshire, met a car whose male occupant leant out of the window and, as he went pass her, yelled the one word: 'Cow!' She naturally took this to be a veiled criticism of her driving, a thing to which she was not unaccustomed, until, rounding a corner, she nearly ran into an agitated Jersey which, escaped from some lush pasture, was lumbering along in the general direction of Wokingham.

We had other motoring friends, the Parmenters, to whom something rather unusual occurred. They owned a car and, behind it, a caravan and, holidaying in Scotland, were proceeding cautiously down a steep hill when they became aware that another caravan was attempting to come past them. Braking sharply, they gave it room and Mrs Parmenter, with a glad cry, said: 'Why just look, Tom! How extraordinary! They've got exactly the same curtains as ours.' Yes, yes, they had indeed. It was their very own caravan which, unhitching itself, had taken on a gladsome life of its own, careered full tilt down the incline and shot, in a mood of joyous abandon, over a stone wall and into a loudly splintering oblivion beyond.

So much for some of one's own experiences but who can doubt that the Under-Secretary's approbation was well founded and also perhaps extended to our road signs, each so individual and British and not always very easy for foreigners to understand.

Picture if you will a male French motorist arriving at Dover and heading for London. Suddenly at the roadside he sees a thrilling notice. It says SOFT VERGES, a challenge indeed to that whiskery and amorous race for the word 'verges' being so very close to the Frog *'vierges'*, he excitedly interprets the words as 'compliant virgins' (such an unexpected treat in the middle of Kent). Hastily drawing up, he scans the countryside for these boons to the weary traveller. Nothing in sight, however, but hop-pickers! But there, *que voulez-vous*? Just Perfidious Albion up to its tricks again.

SIGNAL FAILURE

One sometimes notices things much more sharply when, paradoxically, they aren't there any more. Musing the other day about various matters as I, expecting lunch guests and unmindful of self, prepared an apple charlotte (let me recommend a pound of Lane's Prince Albert which suit it perfectly, coupled with, and layered with, a mixture of four ounces of sugar, three of breadcrumbs and two each of suet and butter, the butter to be applied in dabs, a toothsome recipe which comes to us by involuntary courtesy of *Pears Cyclopaedia*, 1953 edition), I asked myself what on earth has happened, in motoring circles, to hand signals. They apparently exist no more but twenty or so years ago everybody was at it and flapping wildly. ('I am stopping.' 'I am turning left.' 'Kindly pass.') You could always tell a Learner Driver, not merely by the L-plates but by the tremendous elaboration and conscientiousness of his signals, arm right out of the car and wrist fully flexible, not unlike a wonky gentleman saying 'But my *dear*!' Anxious to solve the riddle, and as soon as my charlotte was completed (I forgot to say lemon juice; slosh it on), I rang a reputable Exeter School of Motoring and a kind lady (on the switchboard, I fancy, but fully au fait with the very latest in motorcraft) informed me that hand signals were still being taught and were there, all ready, 'if needed'. No legal compulsion to use them, it seems, and indeed if there were, every motorist would be arrested for negligence eighty-nine times a day.

By the same token (and I always find that a gracious phrase

like that one, with an old-fashioned and courtly ring to it, helps one's prose along no end), I fell to asking myself what those flashing headlights signify when one vast jumbo lorry passes another. Sometimes it is just the one flash, but sometimes it is a jerky series of light explosions reminiscent of the Morse Code, invented by the American, Samuel Morse (information again by courtesy of *Pears*, such a standby for those short on facts) and some time in the mid-nineteenth century. Are the lorry gentlemen urging each other along ('Oh well *driven!*') and arranging to meet for late supper? Is it perhaps 'How's the wife and nippers?' Possibly some of them are more artistically-minded than appearances and their arduous calling might suggest and the jerky flashes mean 'There's Scarlatti on Radio Three,' or 'Who does your hair-styling?' or 'Isn't Dali the complete and absolute *end!*'

Motorists have, of course, cleverly invented a signal of their very own (and who on earth began it? it's like those inventors of Stock Exchange Jokes, and we shall never know) and one which is, I assume, illegal and would certainly be taught by no instructor. It is a valuable signal and it means two things, one pretty well the opposite of the other. I refer to the suddenly illuminated, in daylight, headlamp. This is now in frequent use on long straight stretches of road and is a reprimand given by an approaching car to somebody who has overtaken when there wasn't really room. This single flash says much. ('Now, that was very reckless and dangerous of you, was it not, and I only hope that the lady beside you and in the charming hat is your wife and is going to give you a sensational wigging all the way back to Biggleswade.') On more agreeable occasions, the flash is used to welcome into the main stream of traffic a car waiting patiently in a town's side-street. Here, too, it says so much. ('Do come on in, as I have done my shopping and am in no sort of hurry and I expect you've still got to get to Sainsbury's and the Co-op and then join Bimbo in the Rising Sun for a quickie.')

And speaking of signals and wishing to raise the tone a little after the mention of Drink, what about *Ships that pass in the night*, written by Henry Wadsworth (such solid and suitable names) Longfellow? (How many of you honestly thought, as I did until I looked it up, that it was Kipling?) The poet added that the ships 'speak to each other in passing; only a signal shown and a distant voice in the darkness' and, being Longfellow, he presses on with a gloomy reference to the same sort of thing always happening to human beings on 'the ocean of life' — distant sightings and feeble shouts and then nothing. Rubbish! A good many of the ships that, in life, one has sighted and hailed have slowed down and put out their fenders, or whatever those rope and cord anti-bump things are called, preparatory to coming alongside and, in friendly fashion, letting down their gangways. But trust him to have taken the dreariest view.

I suppose that one of the most apparently anti-social ships in history was the *Californian* which, hove to in Atlantic ice in 1912 and on a night that it is impossible to forget, did absolutely nothing about a very large liner which, also halted and relatively close (twelve or so miles, it seems), appeared to be sending up distress rockets and adopting an unusual angle in the water, before vanishing altogether. To add yet another to the great Ifs of history, what, one wonders, would have happened if the *Titanic*'s Captain Smith had, the moment the ship struck the iceberg at 11.40 pm, lowered a boat manned by the ship's toughest rowers and had ordered them to make, hell for leather, for the *Californian*, whose lights were visible across the totally calm sea? What speed could a ship's boat, with desperate men at the oars, make through the water? Eight knots, perhaps? They might have reached the *Californian* by, say, one am. The *Titanic* had still an hour and twenty minutes to live, time enough, surely, for the *Californian*, even with reduced steam and speed, to arrive on the scene and rescue some of those in the water (it was, they say, the icy cold rather than drowning that did for so many who had had to opt for the sea). There are those who defend, for this or that reason, the

186

Californian's captain, but he does, at the very least, seem to have been rather lacking in curiosity.

The facts about the disaster continue to be both bizarre and endlessly fascinating and some of them are almost beyond belief. There was the gym instructor who, for there was electrical power to the end, tried to get passengers' minds on to something less agitating than the ever increasing slope of the decks by encouraging them to ride the gym's electric horses. At the evening service (disaster day was a Sunday, for those who like to make something of it), the Rev Carter had chosen as the hymn *For Those in Peril on the Sea* but thought it prudent, after the Blessing, to remind the congregation of the splendid steadiness and safety of the ship. It is not at all widely known that the *Titanic* was licensed to carry 3,457 people and was therefore nothing like full (2,201 persons on board), thus avoiding an even more appalling number of deaths and making the completely inadequate yet legal number of lifeboats seem even more disgraceful.

As is perhaps remembered, my admiration for Americans is boundless, but I do have to say that when they go in for bad taste, they do it in a very big way. In 1972 and on the sixtieth anniversary of the tragedy, the 300 members of the *Titanic* Enthusiasts of America saluted the happy event in various ways. One of them was to build a four-foot model of the *Titanic*, together with a papier-mâché iceberg, and float both on a pond. The model was radio-controlled and the idea was to guide it into the iceberg and achieve a sinking. But strong winds defeated the enterprise and, so as not to disappoint onlookers, the ship was scuttled by blowing a hole in her side by remote control. While all this was going on, a Californian fun party was in progress in and around two lifeboats labelled *Titanic*. 'Boat drill scheduled to start at eight o'clock,' ran the invitation, '1912 attire required.' And there has, more recently, been a sick joke on the subject. 'What did the Gilbert and Sullivan fan sing as the *Titanic* went down?' Give up? 'I've Got a Little List.'

WASTE LANDS

As readers of this page, sadly noting, and with a head shake, this or that recurrent manifestation of the writer's personality (a thin thing at the best of times and apt to be, in the long run, as insubstantial as gossamer) will have long since realised, I am dead nuts on Americans. I first met them in bulk and en masse in 1942 when they started to arrive in Northern Ireland, a theatre of war where I, dressed as a somewhat charade-like Captain in the Intelligence Corps, and others had been since 1940 stationed with orders to repel any attempted landing by old Jerry in the South. Information as to how old Jerry was going to transport and maintain a large enough force across the vast and unfriendly seas was not vouchsafed us, for the simple reason that there was no information. And shade our eyes as we might across the briny, never a sign of old Jerry (rather busy in Russia and elsewhere) did we see. I was happy to be in the Intelligence Corps where it was alleged that 'your languages' would come in handy, and I could certainly have said 'Go away!' to an invading enemy in either German or French, but as a Corps its merits did not at first, I regret to say, rank very highly with combative troops, blooded in action. The Intelligence Corps badge represented a small flower (I never did know which or what or why, nestling against a background of foliage) and it was widely known, I am sorry to have to tell you, as 'a pansy resting on its laurels'. One shrugged off the cheap insult.

When the first boatloads of Americans arrived in Belfast, the kindly Irish got out some old and festive bunting by way of welcome and our gallant rescuing cousins from across the pond strode down the gangways and came ashore beneath string upon string of fluttering flags of all nations, among which the Rising Sun was especially prominent. No matter. Too polite to object, the Americans' characters were as open and honest and agreeable as their faces.

In due course, I met many dozens of them and, fully integrated, we worked together, in England and Europe, for three years. It was for me an entirely happy experience. I found them in every way generous. I have since then gone on contentedly meeting Americans. They are an excellent race. Those who think otherwise should just pause and consider where we should all of us be without them (chat about it, amongst yourselves, down the salt mines).

Only in one connection do I get ratty with them. They are one and all extremely wicked about wasting food. With one's perceptions sharpened by the privations that people on the wartime home front endured in the field of comestibles (toothsome Woolton pie and swede cutlets, and not much of either), one was appalled to see that no American ever finished what he had allowed to be put (one can always say 'less, please' or 'thank you, I have a sufficiency') upon his plate. Mounds of meat and tons of spuds were messed about and shoved aside. I have seen cigarettes stubbed out in the mangled remains of a tasty quiche, and although this extraordinary and nationwide lapse was most distressing during a war and in a largely starving world, it is just as unacceptable in peace. For they are still at it. Travelling in America, one still sees a shattering waste (those vast blue oval plates with far too much on them). And, when in England, not even their admirable good manners save them. I have found myself having to apologise to waiters ('Mr and Mrs Wanamaker adored their fish but they both have these little tummy upsets') when my guests' two exquisitely grilled soles have been a quarter eaten and then rejected. So odd that, apart from anything else, they never seem to realise how rude it is. Perhaps my schoolmasterly experiences have made me unduly censorious ('You are not to move from this table, Perryman, until you have finished your blancmange').

These thoughts were prompted, and various dietary memories stirred by an unfortunate incident this very morning. I am at the moment away from 'Myrtlebank' and having a short holiday in Cornwall. Loving hotels with a passion second only to that of my deep emotional feeling for musical comedies of the 1920s and '30s, I always find it difficult to decide where to take myself and my luggage, and on the subject of luggage let me just say that the coloured magazine advertisements' insidious attempts to make me feel small if I don't have at least three matching suitcases 'in handsomely tooled leatherette' have failed. My two canvas bags accompany me everywhere and are as loosely held together as myself. Before setting off, I always consult the best of my wide range of hotel guides, liking to know just where I shall be ('The cosy TV room adjoins the Regency snack bar') and what is what ('There is a special kiddies' playground behind the putting green'). I especially like those guides that tell you of happy happenings upon the author's last visit to the establishment: 'As we sipped our aperitifs in the tastefully appointed cocktail lounge, we were joined by Mine Host, the genial Major E.J.B d'Arcy Bellingham and his cheery wife, Shirleen, who advised us on no account to miss, at dinner, the chef's speciality, *goujons de merluche*, washed down by a chilled St Bernard 1963 (Good for you, Belly. They were both spot on!)'.

Luck was indeed with me in my choice, and I do not only mean an absence of Belly and Shirleen types, though an enormously efficient management lurked. A charming bedroom looked out over a beautifully terraced garden (two dedicated gardeners violently at work) and a richly wooded valley running down to the sea. No TV lounge but my very own coloured set for, with '*Crossroads*' only recently restored to our screens, one would not wish to miss a single sparkling episode (things at the Motel are every bit as dicey as one had feared and the winter advance bookings seem minimal). One's bed got turned down at night, now a rare occurrence, and one's shoes, when put out, got cleaned (rarer still). It was service with a smile all round. Facilities existed for keeping telephonically in touch with the outside world without having to go through the hotel switchboard, an activity that can ('Melinda's gone to her supper') be thwarting. Food of great variety and deliciousness at every meal. After dinner, coffee *ad lib* (no dreary counting of cupfuls) and the run of one's teeth, if I may so phrase it with so few of my resident molars left to me, with the After Eights.

The unhappy incident to which I have referred took place after breakfast. Leaving my table, with a gracious thank-you to the impeccable waitress, and orange juice (fresh), Rice Krispies, grilled kipper, toast, marmalade and coffee circulating digestively within me, I passed a table where I had seen a slightly un-English-looking mother and father and two teenage children recently breakfasting. A scene of truly appalling devastation greeted my troubled and cross (in the sense of angry) eyes. The family had plainly all ordered bacon and sausages and eggs for there, barely touched and pulled about and mucked up, were the terrifying remains. The hotel supplies, in addition to toast, homebaked and delightfully hot bread rolls. Battered rolls were everywhere. Saucers were full of slopped-over coffee. There was cigarette ash in the orange juice. Marmalade dribbled down the side of a pot. A shaming and repellent spectacle. Americans, obviously.

I like, in my pompous way, to say a comforting word whenever it is possible. One may not have another opportunity. 'I shall not pass this way again,' the quotation goes (and perhaps *Oxford* has now finally decided who it was who said it), and thank heaven for that. I have had a wonderful life but not one single second of it would I wish to call back or repeat. Poor old Faust must have been out of his mind. Enough is enough. However, be that as it may, I passed, on my way out of the dining-room, the head waiter, lost in thought. In case his mind had already leapt ahead to lunch and he was wondering whether we would notice that today's savoury rissoles were last night's veal, I drew his attention to the battleground scene at Table Number Five. I tut-tutted over the bacon and clucked disapprovingly over the sausages, and all this by way of showing sympathy for the hotel servants. I threw in a word or two, popular in nursery days, about the starving Chinese, grateful even for crumbs. And I said how sadly typical it was of the otherwise faultless American race. 'Americans? I don't understand. The family at this table comes from Manchester. They come twice a year and we're all very fond of them. And now, if you'll excuse me . . .' Collapse of old buffer but how distressing to discover, and I've seen evidence of it elsewhere, that we are now too, evidently, 'into' disgraceful wastefulness.

LITERARY
RAMBLES

As a boy at school, studying the literary works of the great and long since dead, and I refer to such stodgepots as Ovid, Schiller and Racine, no teacher ever thought to remind us that these august figures, who seemed remote and unbelievable were basically much the same as you and me. I mean, they had two legs, two arms, a head and assorted extras, and with these they ate, slept, yawned, scratched themselves, hiccoughed, made noises and went to the lavatory just like anybody else. This would have made them seem much more real and acceptable, and ditto the characters of whom they wrote.

Now take Shakespeare. It is true that, for dramatic purposes, we see the Macbeths only at crisis points in their lives, but how much cosier would have been a quiet breakfast scene on a morning when no guest happens to have been murdered the night before. I can't speak Scots but I picture Lady Macbeth sounding a bit like dear old Janet in *Dr Finlay's Casebook*. She enters. 'Och, Macbeth, ma dearie, you've no touched yer tatties or buttered one of wee Maggie's baps. Och, ah dinna ken what's got into ye the noo.' She then announces that she's driving over to Perth to order some new whimples and to buy a tin of Rumbold's Antler Polish, and so another happy day begins.

And miles to the south, at Elsinore in Denmark, how would poor old Hamlet be getting on at breakfast? His mother, Queen Gertrude, would of course be in complete charge, a regal figure behind the coffee-pot. Her current husband, King Claudius, hands her a peach. 'Ah, thank you, Claudius. It's

195

been a really superb year for peaches. My first husband, the late king your brother, was himself very fond of a peach. The orchard was full of them — oh Hamlet, for pity's sake don't *twitch* so, you quite startled me, and do munch up your smorgasbord. Now, what time are you and Ophelia playing tennis? And after that you're going bathing? Such a nuisance that that girl can't swim. We must try to arrange some lessons for her. I'm quite sick of watching her just go splosh splosh.'

You see? It just makes all the difference.

READING FOR PLEASURE

I cannot now remember, my mind being so fully stocked with other valuable data, the name of the successful author who confessed that, early on and at one point in his career, he had been able, when in a wild and merry mood, to paper a whole room of his house with the rejection slips sent to him by publishers. Some of these gentlemen, kinder (and with more time) than others, supply, rather than a coldly printed notice of unacceptability, a short letter of regret and explanation, which might go something like this: 'Dear Mr Marshall, In returning to you the manuscript of your novel, *The Strange Quest of Adrian Babbington*, we would like to say that, although the Metropolitan Waterboard background seems to us to be both authentic and finely sketched (we particularly enjoyed the light relief supplied by your crusty old tea-lady, "Mrs H"!) and the chapter in which a leak is discovered in the Staines Reservoir, with the town of Egham put at flood risk, is suspenseful indeed, we rather doubt whether the public is quite ready at the present time for a novel of 250,000 words in which a deprived Waterboard employee struggles to "find himself".'

A friend of mine called Dick decided in the 1920s and after an expensive public school education at healthful and intellectually powerful Malvern College, to stay at home and, in the teeth of strong family opposition and disapprobation, become the writer for whom the world was waiting, providing an endless stream of matchless novels, plays, poems and belles lettres. And accordingly, and working fourteen hours a day, he settled to his task and covered sheet after sheet of paper and, as the manuscripts piled excitingly up on all sides, he sent them here and there for publishers' consideration.

The family lived at Wimbledon and Dick's disapproving father was, as so many in those days were, something in the City and commuted thither every day down the electrified rails. Breakfasting with this forbidding presence morning after morning (his mother wisely had a tray in bed), Dick had to keep his ears cocked for the sound of the postman's boots crunching up the gravel, but however loudly he hummed a tune or clattered dishes or made frenzied conversation, nothing could muffle the gloomy and almost daily thud of a rejected manuscript being pushed through the letter-box and falling heavily to the hall floor. 'What was that, my boy?' his father used to ask, looking up from the *Morning Post*. 'I heard nothing,' Dick lied, scuttling swiftly from the room and hiding the tattered brown paper parcel behind a curtain. He subsequently found, I am happy to say, a cosy and more suitable niche as a play-reader in the world of the theatre, where he was much liked. Like many another, he found it easier and more restful to comment on the literary works of others rather than to have to provide them himself.

The splendid *Woman's Hour* section of the BBC recently took a leaf out of the admirable Roy Plomley's book and ran a series in which contributors were asked to state, with explanations, which six persons, dead or alive, they would choose to have, or *not* to have, with them on a desert island. I was kindly invited to take part and I chose to have Lady Macbeth (obviously, provided you locked your bedroom door, such a splendid hostess and provider of food — Duncan's last dinner must have been perfection for just look how soundly he slept), Christine Truman (the only recent player of brilliance who looked as though she actually enjoyed playing tennis), Shirley Williams (of whom I think very highly as a potential Prime Minister) and Joan Sutherland (in addition to that voice, a tip-top person from down under). And though I mean them nothing but good, I chose not to have Dame Edna (too noisy, and after a week or so we might feel called upon to duck her in the sea and forget to bring her up again) and Mr Heath (I feared that he might wear a yachting cap all day and keep on telling us from which point of the compass the morning clouds were coming).

And so I saw myself, in the long, happy, sun-drenched days, listening to Joan, admiring Shirley, watching Christine practising her serves with a palm frond and a coconut, and waiting for Lady Macbeth to bring in the baked halibut.

I see no reason why Mr Plomley's excellent wheeze should not be elaborated even further and contributors be invited to provide a list of the eight books that, marooned, they would find indispensable. The choice would be almost impossibly difficult and one is torn this way and that, but I myself could not bear long to be parted from *The Enchanted April* by, as she always liked to be called 'the author of *Elizabeth and her German Garden*', first published in 1922, and a book published just thirty years later, namely Rupert Hart-Davis's biography of *Hugh Walpole*. Can there ever have been a wittier, livelier, more tactfully revealing, more wholly fascinating and more agreeably written biography? I very much doubt it. Mr Walpole's (he became Sir Hugh in 1937) is of course, an example of a literary career that was, almost from the start, triumphantly successful, though, as with Somerset Maugham, it did not please all the critics (vast sales and relatively luxurious lives are hard to bear when enjoyed and lived by others). The material to draw on was splendidly copious — diaries, journals, countless letters to and from friends, newspaper cuttings, recollections (he died in 1941, a mere fifty-seven years old) and the fact that the author had enjoyed a close and ten-year friendship with his subject. Their coming-together is as ideal as Gilbert and Sullivan, Marks and Spencer and eggs and bacon.

How many people still read Walpole's books? They would be foolish to omit *Mr Perrin and Mr Traill*, an unexpectedly dramatic theme partly based on the author's odd schoolmastering experiences at Epsom College, and this book, coupled with *The Dark Forest* and *The Old Ladies*, would give a novice a good idea of Walpole's abilities. To try him out again for myself, I re-read the first eighty pages of *Rogue Herries* which I had not looked at since it first appeared in 1930. Did I want to go on? Indeed I did. With its splendidly readable story and its absence of demanding intellectual matter, it is just my style, though it and its author were much mocked at the time.

Sir Rupert does not mock. He lovingly teases instead, and indeed there is much in Sir Hugh to tease — the wild and boyish enthusiasms, the lists at the year's end of My Best Friends in order of preference, the tiffs about nothing, his joy in his possessions (his Polperro house, 'The Cobbles', was known to Arnold Bennett as 'The Collywobbles'), the resentment of criticism and his delight in knowing what is called 'Everybody'. There was also in him a strong element of Mr Pooter and our author merrily recounts the many occasions when things did not go quite right. Mr Walpole went to the Chelsea Arts Ball. 'Great fun only my trousers split.' Hardly had he alighted at the Lido in 1921 when, on his way to one of the Turkish baths where he appreciated the social informalities possible among clouds of steam, his pocket was picked and his wallet stolen. Improbably in Russia in 1915 and nobly succouring the wounded, 'I lost my braces.' If he boarded a bus, he left on it his suitcase full of dress clothes. Leaving for America, he was found to have neither ticket nor visa. He was apt to come purlers in the Tottenham Court Road. In Liverpool he (a) fell off the dock, and (b) 'the back of my bags split.'

There are two very engaging things about him — his immense financial generosity (he was one of those who do endless good in secret) and his almost constant high spirits. His greatly revered Henry James wrote to him in a pre-August 1914 to confess 'aged, impotent envy of your *joie de vivre*' and, although one always resents the fact that our phrase for such an agreeable matter has to be in French, one sees what the Master means. Sir Hugh was swept along on a torrent of good humour and happiness, and that is very pleasing to read about. Rather rare, too.

BUMPS IN THE NIGHT

Before I state, loudly and clearly, that I don't really believe in ghosts, I have something to confess.

As a public schoolboy in the ancient town of Oundle in Northamptonshire, I lived in a boarding-house in the town itself and our way to the majority of the school buildings lay past the beautiful parish church and then through the churchyard, long since disused and jammed to bursting point with the venerable dead (such *names* one saw on the mossy headstones: Jeremiah Titman, Oswald Blackthorn, Silas Barleycorn, and so on). This particular journey was about 300 yards long and the path wound its way in and out around grassy graves dotted with evergreens. In company and in daylight, the trip meant nothing. In company and at night, with only two modestly-powered gaslamps lighting the way, the journey was less enjoyable. At night and alone, returning perhaps from a music lesson or extra coaching in algebra, the journey was indeed a nightmare.

There was no escaping it, for we were forbidden to go round through the town unless bent on shopping, and shopping for us ended at 2.30 pm. And within the churchyard there was no escape, for a high stone wall kept one to the path on one side, and spiked railings did the same on the other. There was nothing for it but to press on. One whistled, one sang, one rattled one's music-case along the railings for company, but none of this made a ha'porth of difference. I was scared.

Nothing and nobody ever turned up. Titman and Barleycorn stayed where they were, underground. No ghostly shapes loomed though, if the night were at all misty, vaporous wreaths of whiteness took on odd outlines and sometimes made me long to break into a run. But I resolutely walked, fearing cowardice even more than the ghosts in which I don't truly believe. And though I saw nothing, and heard nothing, and believed nothing, I have to say that, despite all this, I sensed that there was SOMETHING THERE. But what or which or how or why, who can say?

There are many persons who are only too ready to button-hole you and, with eyes every bit as glittering as those of that dreadful old Ancient Mariner, claim to have seen ghosts. And usually not just the one ghost. Several ghosts. They seem to take a hearty pride in their acquaintance with ghosts. But if I happened to have a ghost as a chum and, say, Oswald Blackthorn occasionally dropped in, wearing a see-through sheet, for elevenses, I would keep extremely quiet about it, for it never seems to have occurred to anybody before to mention the fact that ghosts are, one and all, totally useless bores.

It is true that, for a cheap party trick, they can walk through walls, but then what? They stare at the moon and moan. They wring their hands. They give off strange, musty smells. When the mood is on them, they twang harps. They wink in an alarming manner. They take off their heads. They glide about as though on wheels. They stand on staircases and get in people's way. They tend to dress in blue gauze and wear squeaky boots. They twitch nervously and cause draughts. Do they ever mow the lawn or tackle the washing-up or run up a batch of tasty rock-cakes? No they do not. And if they have the slightest scrap of interesting news from the Other Side (Cleopatra has taken up golf; Mozart beat Rasputin in the handicap tennis final) they take care to keep it to themselves.

Ghosts in fiction are, unfortunately, a good bit more chatty than those in real life, and one of them was a really frightful old gas-bag. I am referring, of course, to Hamlet's father, given to wearing somewhat showy suits of armour which must have clanked very disagreeably as he moped round the Elsinore

202

battlements. I wouldn't mind betting that he had his medals on as well.

This ghost did have, I suppose, a justifiable grievance. I do see that to be the King and then to be poisoned in an orchard by one's brother after lunch while taking a short forty-winks' rest in a deck-chair from the taxing demands of affairs of state, isn't a thing that happens to everybody and could come as a shock, but on the other hand he really does make rather a meal of it and his advanced melancholia and vengeful attitude are far from pleasing. And then, just as we think we've got rid of him and he's said: 'Adieu!' several times, he starts shouting up through the castle floorboards and making everybody jump.

I must, however, be grateful to the ghost of Hamlet's father for one thing. I have written before of the delightful oddities and weird-sounding flights of fancy of the Dutch language. Friends of mine who have, recklessly perhaps, witnessed a performance of *Hamlet* in Amsterdam, assure me that, when the English line: 'I am thy father's spirit' occurs, what you hear the actor say in Dutch is: 'Ik ben de Poppaspook.' They further add that the name Hamlet seems to come out as Omlet. But they may be pulling my leg.

While we're on Shakespeare, let me say that, for a real sense of decorum and a tactful approach to life, Banquo's ghost would be hard to beat. Banquo, too, as you'll recall, had good grounds for complaint, being a fellow-general of Macbeth's who happened to know, or suspect, too much and got hacked to pieces by no fewer than three hired assassins (trust the Macbeths not to do things by halves) and was left, dead, in a ditch. By way of a mild protest at this questionable conduct, all Banquo then does is to appear in ghost form at the Palace at Forres at the singularly ill-advised Banquet 'thrown' by the new royalties, both of them vulgarly appearing in fully regal robes and showing off like mad (Macbeth's assurance to the guests that he is merely 'playing the humble host' deceives nobody).

203

Banquo shows throughout what a gentleman he is by observing the old nursery instruction to children, 'If you can't think of anything nice to say, don't say anything at all.' He remains politely mum, though the temptation to come out with an angry 'I say, look here!' must have been great. I cannot see why Macbeth should get so agitated at the sight of him. He certainly sits down in Macbeth's seat, and just as everybody, forks raised, is about to tuck in, but there is obviously bags of room for all. Banquo had anyway been warmly bidden to the feast, and if his ghost turns up instead, what of it? This was the moment, if ever there was one, for a display of manly calm on the part of the host and the carrying out of his hospitable and pleasurable duties ('Come, Lennox, let me press you to another devilled kidney.')

As to earthly attempts to reach an imaginary spirit world, it's each man to his own wishes and beliefs. If people can fool themselves that they've 'got through', and if it then brings them real help and comfort, well and good. I have never attended a séance and really it is just as well. I have all my life been troubled by a tendency to laugh on almost any occasion. Frivolous, I know, but there it is. I know full well that the subdued lights, the heavy breathing, the jargon ('Mrs Henderson-Whyte is now in trance'), the loud table raps (the best mediums have, I'm told, double-jointed knees and can cheerfully rap in almost any circumstances), the serious faces, and shufflings behind the scenes, would all do for me and I should collapse into hysteria. I should cause offence and unhappiness, which I don't like doing.

And I feel sure that the whole charade would remind me all too vividly of *Blithe Spirit* and Madame Arcati and the heavenly Margaret Rutherford arriving breathless on that bicycle and swallowing a hasty dry martini before getting down to work. There is too, I gather, at séances a danger of getting suddenly covered in ectoplasm. Ectoplasm, I understand, is a substance that is alleged to 'emanate' from mediums, and its composition and purpose both seem to be complete mysteries. The dictionary's definition is vague and guarded in the extreme. Ectoplasm may, of course, be all right in its way, like blancmange, but all I can say is that it doesn't *sound* very all right.

BROWN STUDIES

In a wholesome spirit of sartorial self-criticism and a plucky determination to face facts and to see things and myself as they truly are, I have to confess that I am possibly a trifle inclined, when out of doors, to wear my macintosh on almost all occasions and in all weathers, fair and foul. Not for me your skimpy modern waterproof which comes to an end a foot or so above the knee, sends the rain water cascading down and seems especially designed to soak the lower halves of trousers. When, three years ago, I decided to throw financial caution to the winds and to splash out on a new mac, I had some difficulty in locating one of sufficient length to protect my knees. The lips of London sellers of such garments curled in contempt at my old-fashioned request for a really lengthy macintosh and these supercilious *vendeurs* were much astonished when, to their parrot cries of: 'There's no demand for them these days,' I wittily countered with 'Well, you have a demand now.' Eventually, and it is one more reason for admiring Devon, I ran one to earth in an Exeter boutique that caters for the sedate male middle-aged and, thus protectively kitted out, I have been wearing my mac more or less continuously ever since and moving freely about among the public, not exactly the cynosure of all eyes but just a humble chap and one of the crowd, don't you know.

Or so I thought until a really startling occurrence of a few weeks ago catapulted me and my togs into an enviable prominence. This totally unexpected happening took place on a Sunday and, so I like to think, in my devout way, that the pleasing event was perhaps, if not actually inspired, at least blessed from Above. Here are the details. I do not know which, if any, Sunday newspaper you read (or how, in some of them, you ever manage to find your way through the various sections to the item of your choice) but the one of which I write is a highly reputable sheet, if a little inclined, so lavish are they with the printers' ink, to make the hands grubby, a misfortune that a mere two-minute session with luxuriously foaming Camay puts instantly to rights. This newspaper lists, of course, the day's television attractions, if such they may all be called, and on this particular day it announced, at 7.15 pm, the usual weekly programme of *Call My Bluff*, and there, for all to see and goggle at, were the words '. . . with the elegant addition of . . .' followed by my name. Did you ever! I have waited nearly seventy years to be called 'elegant' and I mean to enjoy and treasure every moment of this verbal accolade.

But what can have caused this? Puzzling my brains, and liking to give credit where credit is indeed due, I put the whole thing down to my new suit from the Army & Navy Stores. This, a form-hugging uncrushable two-piece in, it says, '45% Virgin Wool' and bearing a label proudly saying that it was MADE IN YUGOSLAVIA, has been displayed twice on television and has clearly caught the public eye and the public fancy and the public imagination. Just in the very unlikely case of your not having yet seen it, you'll probably like to know its colour: something between a darkish buff and a lightish fawn, with a bit of beige and milk chocolate thrown in. Brown, in fact, and defiantly I say it, flying in the critical face of whoever it was — Evelyn Waugh, possibly — who said that no gentleman, which one struggles so hopelessly to be, could ever conceivably be seen, alive or dead, clothed in brown. Seated at a table as we are for this telly programme, it is only on the top half of me that viewers can feast their eyes and so I could, if I were dishonest, cheat and wear, programme after programme, a pair of all-purpose grey bags from, where else, Marks and Spencer. But I do not cheat and those viewing my brown top half can rest assured that I am, so to speak, brown all over.

But if my suit has, in general, been pretty widely admired, I have to say that the adjective brown has some associations that are very far from being delightful. Although it now seems, thank goodness, to have gone out of fashion and features decreasingly on hotel menus, time was when no evening repast in an ill-lit and musty dining-room was considered complete without Brown Windsor soup, a gloomy liquid that was all too clearly surplus gravy from the last three days' joints, eked out with water, thickened with flour and heated to room temperature. One lapped it up, crumbling a stale roll, just prior to the sad-faced waiter shuffling morosely forward to say that the beef was off, the word 'off' here meaning 'available no longer' or 'all gobbled up', rather than off-colour or 'high', though both meanings must have been, on occasion and in hot weather, applicable. If the soup, which has a Victorian sound to it, originated in Windsor itself and, as one supposes, amongst the very highest in the land, it was doubtless heavily fortified with good bone stock and enriched with the finest sherry so that pleasingly fruity aromas ('Come, my dear, another ladleful?') hung about the Prince Consort's whiskers, until bedtime and a final going-over with a face flannel removed them (the aromas).

Further disagreeable brown associations are provided by the dreaded Brownshirts, hateful Hitler's storm-troopers who helped to raise him to a peak of evil that makes the Kaiser seem like Little Nell, and also by a, to me, unacceptable phrase. It was, I think, early in the last (and would it were) War that I became aware of people saying dejectedly that they were browned off, meaning fed up or bored or both. Apart from the fact, irritating though it may be to others, that I have never in my life been bored (there is always *something* to shriek or marvel at) and only very seldom fed up, I consider it an ugly-sounding phrase originating, I can only think, in the kitchen, and perhaps an American kitchen at that ('Mary

Lou's just browning off her cookies'.)

Poets have been noticeably loth to use the word brown. One searches in vain in the works of Burns for a reference to, perhaps, 'Ma bonnie wee brown Mary', brown here implying a healthily sun-tanned lassie who has caught the poet's wildly roving eye while she was, maybe, coming unaccompanied through the rye, hardly a recommendable perambulation with a certain Scotsman about or, if you prefer it, aboot. Poor old Tennyson, maundering away in the Isle of Wight and markedly listless (statistics show the area to be even more climatically relaxing than palm-strewn Torquay), certainly refers, in *A Dream of Fair Women* to 'A queen with swarthy cheeks', and though swarthy indicates dark-skinned, it is dark-skinned verging on black and very far from being brown. And then back he hurries to 'a daughter of the gods, divinely tall and most divinely fair', and although 'fair' can indeed just mean beautiful, who can doubt that it is imaginary blonde bombshells that the Laureate has got himself so excited about.

Or was it? I have for some time now had a theory about this poem. It is well known that in Tennyson's day, the summer months in and around Ventnor were greatly enlivened by the presence of swings and roundabouts and giant racers and dodgems — fairs, in fact. Presiding over the hoop-la stall, with one of them due any moment to be promoted to the Fat Lady booth, I seem to see two buxom beauties, Agnes Parker and her sister Doris, drumming up custom with shouts of 'Four hoops a penny' and reluctantly handing out the prizes (barbola-work vases). The poet, on one of his endless tramps across the island, spots them and is instantly captivated by their coarse charms, both of them brown as berries — an infatuation which he had, naturally, to conceal and mask with references to Queen Elizabeth and others. But as he wrote out the poem's title, *A Dream of Fair Women*, even that austere figure may have permitted himself a tiny and lascivious chuckle.

WATER WATER EVERYWHERE

In the country of frozen pipes and dripping ceilings and when icicles hang by the wall, it is the plumber, one-eyed or not, who is king and who must, whether one's water be currently in solid or in liquid form, be rightly bowed down to. In shivering Britain he at once becomes a figure of much greater interest and attraction (no very difficult feat) than any politician.

I find that I can stomach my own bodily misfortunes and weaknesses and malfunctions much more easily than I can bear those that afflict any mechanical contraptions and household amenities that I possess. Cars that will not start, fridges that fail to fridge, sullenly inactive immersion heaters and pipes that burst induce in me a state of panic and desperation. When I am in any way agitated, my voice, already highish, wails up an octave or two like a wartime siren, and overworked plumbers, listening at the other end of a telephone wire, hardly know what to make of me. ('I'll try to squeeze you in this afternoon, Madam.')

In my youth, jovial grown-ups who required at mealtimes a glass of water from the jug used often to say: 'Bung along the H_2O, there's a good chap' but nowadays water has become almost an object of reverence. How odd that such a simple substance should in recent years have demanded such an abundant recruitment of officials to look after it. Here in the south west where I live, you can now hardly move down a Devon lane without coming upon a small van labelled either WATER or WATERBOARD. During the bad drought, old ladies naturally thought that WATER meant 'supplies of' and, pressing forward with empty plastic buckets, hammered hopefully on the doors.

No water or anything useful like that was forthcoming and so we all wondered what on earth the occupants of these official vehicles could be up to. Were they down on their knees and praying wildly for rain? Were they studying the cloud formations? Can they have seized their hazel-twigs and were eagerly water-divining on the surrounding hills? Whatever they were doing, or not doing, water seems to become every year more expensive and, down here, rarer. In September, a mere two days without rain caused requests to us all to go carefully with this precious fluid.

Water looms large, of course, in literature's pages, particularly those of Shakespeare, and, with no Waterboard to bother it, was always ready to hand. Lady Macbeth, ever the practical housewife, urges its use while tidying up after Duncan's unfortunate mishap ('the servants were responsible, you know'). 'Too much of water hast thou' cries Laertes (he wouldn't today) after his sister Ophelia's watery demise and I must, by the way, confess that I have never been too happy about the exact circumstances surrounding the mysterious death by drowning of this winsome Danish fiancée and the bespoken princess of Hamlet in the play of that name. The coroner, it is true, brought in a verdict of misadventure and added suitable commiserations with the bereaved relatives (rather few on the ground by then and, indeed, a no-parent family, following the death of Ophelia's father, Polonius, in an alleged fencing accident). I have a suspicion — and they may care to insert such a scene in the next production at the National — that Hamlet, seeing what a crackpot the girl had become and anxious not to introduce a further strain of insanity into the royal house (Queen Gertrude is manifestly unbalanced), coaxed her ('Come dear, how about a quick dip?') into the brook and held her, an early Bride in the Bath, down.

I have a theory, its truth borne out by experience, that

'better really means worse', and in matters additional to water. When our splendid police force decided to abandon both walking and bicycling, draped themselves in walkie-talkie wires and other electrical devices and moved about solely in motor-cars, the crime rate instantly trebled itself. When the equally splendid National Westminster Bank decided to erect the biggest bank building in London, or Britain, or the world for all I know, I felt sure that little good would come of it to the customer. Sure enough, with the building half way up, it was decided not to open the banks to customers on a Saturday (still a grave inconvenience for many). And with the building finally and triumphantly completed, I received a communication to the effect that my used cheques could no longer be returned to me (I found them helpful) with my monthly statement as being too exhausting an undertaking administratively.

And so now I'm apprehensive about the Waterboard. The moment I find those vans stuffed with freshly recruited personnel and nose to tail in our lanes, I shall know that this means a gradual drying up of the water supply, a situation that, I must confess, in our present either frozen or dripping circumstances, I can face more calmly than usual. ('Bert will be with you first thing tomorrow, Madam.')

ROYAL MAIL

19 Tregunter Crescent, W8

Your Majesty,

After much hesitation I am taking the liberty of writing to you to ask a favour on behalf of my daughter, Penelope. Young Penny, a well developed twelve-year-old, has recently 'taken up' tennis and has visions of becoming a second Christine Truman! There are no courts at her Comprehensive, though promised, and she 'makes do' in the park.

On my way to and from work (at the Army & Navy Stores) my bus takes me between Victoria and Hyde Park Corner and past the Palace gardens. These have always intrigued me and from the top of the bus one gets a lovely view. With the leaves off the trees, your hard tennis court becomes very clear. It looks in perfect condition, with everything at the ready and the net up, but I have never seen anyone playing on it. Would it be possible, I wonder, for my Penny to make use of it?

Yours sincerely,
Pamela Johnston

From the Lady Jean Sidebotham
Buckingham Palace, SW1

Dear Mrs Johnston,

Her Majesty has commanded me to answer your letter and to say that she regrets that she does not feel able at the present time to agree to your request.

Yours sincerely,
Jean Sidebotham
Lady-in-Waiting to Her Majesty

Dear Lady Sidebotham,

There seems to be some misunderstanding. I was not expecting that Her Majesty would be able to play with Penny, she is clearly much too busy. My daughter would bring along one of her friends. Of course, if Her Majesty would care for a knock-up during a slack time in State affairs, that would be a marvellous bonus!

Penny and her friend would bring their own tennis balls. Their best days would be Tuesday or Friday about 2.30 pm. They are both very excited at the possibility.

Yours sincerely
Pamela Johnston

Dear Mrs Johnston,

Your further letter has been considered and it is regretted that no exception can be made in this case.

Yours sincerely,
Jean Sidebotham

20 Tregunter Crescent, W8

Dear Queen,

My good friend and neighbour, Mrs Johnston, has been telling me how you are planning to be throwing open your tennis courts to youngsters. This is being great good news. My daughter, Helga, 'caught the tennis bog' while staying with her Onkel Heinrich in Hanover last summer and would also like to join up with the group.

Hullo!
Gertrud Bauscher

Dear Mrs Bauscher,

Her Majesty has commanded me to answer your letter and to

say that she is sorry that you have been misinformed and that the tennis court cannot be liberated for public use.

Yours sincerely,
Jean Sidebotham

Dear Lady Sidebotham,
I understand that Mrs Bauscher has written, it was foolish of me to let her into our little secret. Of course if you extend the invitation to everybody the court would become impossibly over-crowded and this is the last thing we want. When would it be convenient for the children to start to play?

Yours sincerely,
Pamela Johnston

Dear Mrs Johnston,
I would very much like to be more helpful but it will be clear to you that the question of security is, in these sad days, of paramount importance and this, if for no other reason, prevents us giving your daughter access to the Palace grounds.

Yours sincerely,
Jean Sidebotham

Dear Lady Sidebotham,
You need have no fear about security. Penny knows better than to damage any trees or shrubs in the garden. We have always brought her up to respect other people's property. Did I spot a side-door to the Palace, which the children could use? It's in that wall near to where dear old Gorringes used to be. If the children were to use that there would be less chance of outsiders getting to know what was going on. They would be

215

careful to stick to the path once inside the Palace grounds. What about next Friday?

Yours sincerely,
Pamela Johnston

Dear Lady Sidebotham,

I am not understanding why Helga's tickets for the court have not come through. Penny Johnston is cock-a-hop all over the Crescent and nothing for Helga! Is this being British Justice?

Hullo!
Gertrud Bauscher

Dear Mrs Bauscher,

I am afraid that you are under a misapprehension. No tickets are being issued to anybody for Her Majesty's hard tennis court. The question of security is, these sad days, of paramount importance.

Yours sincerely,
Jean Sidebotham

Dear Lady Sidebotham,

We Germans are not fearful persons. We mind little of security. A true German is as secure on tennis court as on battlefield. Helga fears nothing. She has her karate medal and can protect herself.

Hullo!
Gertrud Bauscher

Dear Lady Sidebotham,

I wonder if you can have received my last letter. The children are 'all set' — and no news! Next week will be half term and an ideal moment for the children's first visit. Please let me know soon.

Yours sincerely,
Pamela Johnston

From the Hon. Mrs J.C.B. Tynte
Buckingham Palace, SW1

Dear Mrs Johnston,
Lady Jean is away from duty at the moment with a complete nervous breakdown and, in her absence, I am dealing with her letters. As the volume of incoming correspondence is always very great, it is not the Palace practice to retain many letters from the public, or our answers to them, and so I am in some doubt about the 'first visit' to which you refer. Could you please explain?

Yours sincerely,
Muriel Tynte
Lady-in-Waiting to Her Majesty

Dear Mrs Tynte,
Certainly. My daughter, Penelope, has recently 'taken up' tennis . . .

THE CROOKED BAT

Crooked meaning not straight: not crooked meaning dishonest. It always seemed to me, as a schoolboy reluctantly playing cricket in the 1920s, that a straight bat, so highly prized by the experts, was in my case mere foolishness, sending the ball, when I managed to make contact with it, feebly back whence it had come. With a crooked bat there was at least a chance of deflecting the offensive weapon either to right or left and scoring a 'run'. To attempt to score anything at all may savour of self-advertisement but that was never my aim. My sights were not set on a ribboned coat or a captain's hand on my shoulder smote. The sole purpose of a run was to remove me, however briefly, from the end where the action was.

Cricket was a manly game. Manly masters spoke of 'the discipline of the hard ball'. Schools preferred manly games. Games were only manly if it was possible while playing them to be killed or drowned or, at the very least, badly maimed. Cricket could be splendidly dangerous. Tennis was not manly, and if a boy had asked permission to spend the afternoon playing croquet he would have been instantly punished for his 'general attitude'. Athletics were admitted into the charmed lethal circle as a boy could, with a little ingenuity, get impaled during the pole-vault or be decapitated by a discus and die a manly death. Fives were thought to be rather tame until one boy ran his head into a stone buttress and got concussion and another fainted dead away from heat and fatigue. Then everybody cheered up about fives. The

219

things to aim at in games were fright and total exhaustion. It was felt that these, coupled with a diet that was only modestly calorie-laden, would keep our thoughts running along the brightest and most wholesome lines. As a plan, this was a failure.

For cricket matches against other schools, the school pavilion was much in evidence. At my preparatory school, Stirling Court on the Hampshire coast, the pavilion smelt strongly of linseed oil and disinfectant and for its construction reliance had been largely placed on corrugated iron. Within could be found cricket nets and spiders and dirty pads and spiders and old team photographs and old spiders. There was also a bat signed by Hobbs which we proudly displayed to opposing players in an unconscious spirit of gamesmanship. But despite this trophy, a sad air of failure and decay pervaded the building. From its windows innumerable cricketing disasters had been witnessed: for example, our defeat by Dumbleton Park when our total score had been eight, three of which were byes. There had been, too, the shaming afternoon when our captain, out first ball, had burst into a torrent of hysterical tears.

But cricket did have one supreme advantage over football. It could be stopped by rain. Every morning at prayers, devout cricket-haters put up a plea for a downpour. As we were in England, our prayers were quite frequently answered, but nothing, nothing but the death of the headmaster could stop football. We could hardly pray for the headmaster, a nice man, to die. In rain, sleet, hail and lightning, shivering and shuddering and soaked to the skin, we battled on. Even in dense fog we kept at it, a shining example to Dartmoor working parties. But cricket was another matter, cricket was a more sensitive affair altogether, and if, as I fear, there is cricket in heaven, there will also, please God, be rain.

When the dread moment arrived and our side went in, I found myself, low down on the list, actually at the wicket and taking guard ('Leg stump, please'), and positively holding a bat. But held straight or crooked, sooner or later there would come the musical sound of skittling pegs and flying bails and I could remove myself and my pad and sit down. And once safely installed on a rug by the hedge and more or less out of sight, day-dreams took over.

I was badly stage-struck and many of my strange fancies consisted of meetings with Beatrice Lillie, Jack Buchanan and Gertrude Lawrence, all of them brightly dazzling stars whose personalities seemed infinitely more winning than those of the lacklustre adults with whom the expensive school fees were currently requiring one to associate. I gave Miss Lawrence tea at the Carlton on many occasions.

Tea, Miss Lawrence?
Yes, please.
Milk, Miss Lawrence?
Yes, please.
Sugar, Miss Lawrence?
Four lumps, please.

When in course of time and much later in life, this particular daydream turned into reality, I was in no way surprised. I had become quite accustomed to the idea.

Tea, Miss Lawrence?
Yes please, dear.
Milk, Miss Lawrence?
Good God no!
Sugar, Miss Lawrence?
Don't be silly, darling! All I ask is that you should not be *silly*!

At Stirling Court there was an even more improbable daydreamer than I, a remarkable boy called Williamson. He liked to pretend that he was the King, *a* King, any old King, graciously living incognito among us, and firmly incognito he looked with his blazer and grey shorts and grubby knees. It was possible to make him happy for hours by suddenly popping out from behind a tree and yelling 'Sire, Sire, I bring grievous news. Thirty of our stoutest bottoms have foundered off Gravesend.' There was then half a minute's pause for silent laughter. No schoolboy of twelve in those unsophisticated days was proof against the word 'bottom', even when signifying ship. Then Williamson would draw himself up to his full three foot eight and shriek in a piercing treble, 'Then go build ye fifty more, an' Sherwood Forest be stripped bare.'

Sometimes we invented a royal disaster so terrible and calamitous — suicide of the Queen, perhaps, theft of the Crown Jewels, bubonic plague at Westminster — that even Williamson was taken aback and could find nothing more regal to say than a dejected 'Oh *dear!*' On the soccer field, Williamson liked to play centre forward. He was King Harry leading us at Agincourt and bravely did we follow him, deep and offside into the enemy ranks with loyal shouts of 'God for Harry, England, Saint George and Williamson!' You would be right in thinking that we did not win a great many of our school matches.

When I was not day-dreaming myself into Shaftesbury Avenue, the existence or otherwise of a Supreme Being caused some perplexing youthful thoughts. Why, if God were All Good and All Powerful and All Sufficient, did he need to be quite so constantly Thanked? And Thanked for what seemed, as we gazed at the uninspiring, unchanging Sunday lunch, somewhat meagre blessings. In the season of mists and mellow fruitfulness, the mellow fruitfulness that most often came our way was beetroot. It did appear that, in comparison with God's other conjuring tricks, beetroot must rank as a minor achievement, especially when closely associated with vinegar.

And what was God up to? Why did my prayers (Freak Earthquake Destroys School) go completely unanswered? There was not even a disquieting rumbling sound to indicate that I had got through. Jesus seemed more approachable and I felt differently about Him, in spite of a daringly outspoken friend who pointed out that Christ had never had to undergo two of the most testing of human experiences, marriage and parenthood. Maintaining that there was no reason whatever to imagine Christ as devoid of humour, he invented a terrible pair of rude and undisciplined children for Him, Cynthia and Roland Christ, who roared about on motor-bicycles, got into every imaginable teenage pickle, and became a byword in Joppa.

At most schools in the '20s there was never any question of being let off cricket. The thought of asking not to play it never entered anybody's head. If it had, the consequences, at a public school anyhow, were clearly foreseeable. Suppose, let us say, a poetically-minded boy had announced that he wished to spend the afternoon writing an ode, he would have been immediately beaten (four strokes) by the Head of the House. Poetry was unhealthy stuff. Look at Byron. If the poet had been more specific and had said that he wanted to write an Ode to the Matron ('Oh Matron, when with grizzled head half bent with care, sweet ministrant of salve and unguent, breasting thy way defiant bust worn high . . .'), he would have been beaten (six strokes) by the Housemaster, and the poor (certainly) innocent (probably) Matron would have found herself writing to the scholastic agents, Chitty and Gale, for a new situation ('. . . said to have pleasant personality . . . prepared take sole charge . . . excellent "mixer" . . .'). If the embryo Shelley had said that he wished to write an Ode to the Captain of Cricket ('Oh Dennis, when with auburn head half bent with care . . .'), expulsion would have been considered, this extreme measure being subsequently watered down, after an infinity of scowls and threats, to a beating (eight strokes) by the Headmaster. These ceremonies used to take place at 9 pm, the Headmaster sporting a dinner-jacket and being freshly vitamin-charged. The beatings were done, as usual, in the spirit of this hurts me more than you, which was said to be plenty.

When blessed rain had made the cricket pitches too sodden for activity, the obvious alternative, inactivity, was not permitted. We were herded together in the gymnasium. Sometimes there was boxing, that hideous and useless

223

invention. Sometimes there was a pastime called Figure Marching. In Indian file we followed each other round strange geometrical figures, crossing and criss-crossing as instructed and forming patterns which would, no doubt, have looked pretty and interesting from a helicopter hovering above. It was before the days of helicopters.

More often than not, Physical Jerks were our lot, an unfortunate name implying as it does fits and starts and jolts and dislocations. The brochures which dealt with this form of exercise were copiously and incomprehensibly diagrammed. Dotted and arrowed lines and Fig. 6 seemed to prescribe patently absurd contortions. The instructors who steered us through them had chests like pouter-pigeons, crimson-veined faces and army connections. At the end of the lesson, it wasn't the done thing to invite the class quietly to stow away the medicine balls and falling mats that we had been using. Even this simple action had to have a military aura — 'Mats away, *GO!* Balls away, *GO!*'

Though a crooked bat was frowned upon, to use the wrong, two-sides-of-a-triangle side was considered definitely illegal. Following my ingenious plan of deflecting the ball to one side or the other and then getting the hell out of it, I once made use of this wrong side of the bat and brought down upon myself a stream of abuse. The myth that this was, somehow, a dishonest practice, was one of many myths then current in schools:

— If you had a cracked lip and drank from a chipped cup, you would at once catch a disease that was as unmentionable as it was difficult to spell.
— The Eton College Officers' Training Corps was not allowed to wear the King's regulation khaki uniform as they had once, at an OTC camp, bayoneted a boy to death. On Field Days didn't they turn out and turn up in a slightly outré pinkish material of their own devising? Well, then!
— Cold water came to the boil more quickly than hot water.
— Any actress employed upon the musical-comedy stage could be

employed in a more private role for a sum of not less than fifty pounds. Didn't this vast extra intake of money explain those sumptuous-looking country houses in the soggier sections of the Thames Valley, and the photographs that went with them ('Off duty! Bimbo and self redesigning the bog garden.')?

At cricket there was never any thought of excusing those unfortunate enough to wear glasses. It was pre-contact lens days and short-sighted boys left their spectacles in their blazers in the pavilion. They stood, when batting, blinded by the sun and enfeebled by cruel Nature, peering uncertainly up the pitch in a hopeless attempt to see whence Nemesis was coming. They had to rely heavily on their other senses. Their sense of hearing supplied the thud and thunder of the bowler's cricketing boots, the wicket-keeper's heavy breathing (now coming from a lower angle as he crouched down in readiness) and the disagreeable whistling sound of the ball itself which indicated that it had been released and was on its way. Their sense of smell supplied the wind-borne unpleasantnesses of hot flannel, hot sock, hot boy, all of minimal value as directional guides. And their sense of touch told them, sharply and painfully, that the ball had arrived.

And here there was an unfairness. The boys in the First and Second XIs, fully sighted and well able to protect themselves, were provided with a contraption called a 'box', a snug and reinforced padded leather compartment worn about the crutch and into which they tucked, I assume, whatever came most easily to hand. It would have been considered a gross impertinence for any lesser player to plead for this protection. In the lower echelons, our genitals were expendable.

Fashions in cricket change like any others. At Stirling Court the important thing was what the ball would do when it struck the ground. It could go right or go left. It could do nothing special, or it could hit a tuft and shoot sharply upwards, a most unnerving ball. I understand, however, that nowadays the only matter of interest is what the ball does in the air. It seems that it 'swings' this way or that, though I cannot, alas, bring myself greatly to care.

It is sad but true that most of the best schoolboy cricketers of my day paid for their ephemeral glories with a lifetime of mediocrity. Cricketing fame can be fleeting. Who, for example, still remembers that Amy Johnson had one of her front teeth broken by a cricket ball and that she was the only girl at the Boulevard Secondary School, Hull, who could bowl over-arm?

Nothing was stranger at preparatory schools in the 1920s than the way in which a sudden spree was visited on the inmates. Without a word of warning, everybody up-anchored and shot off to somewhere else. At Stirling Court one summer's day a special treat was announced. We were all to go by charabanc, as a bus was then called, to watch a professional cricket match at Portsmouth. The outing meant, at least, no school work and even the more anti-cricket boys were in merry mood as we clambered on board. Williamson and I, deep in chat as was our custom, settled ourselves in. We were only mildly surprised to observe that the expedition was not being led by the games master but by a strangely-scented rotundity who taught Latin, was said to debauch the maids and pawn confiscated penknives, and survived but one shaky term. Off we went and on reaching the ground it was apparent that the game had been in progress for some time. Philip Mead, of whom even I had heard, was batting.

When we had found our seats, our first concern, after the hour's drive, was to make for the lavatory, an open-air and rather whiffy square construction of brick, conveniently close. As we hastened in, a solitary figure drew all eyes. In a corner, and facing outwards, an aged and decrepit clergyman was standing, smiling encouragement and wildly waggling. At our fairly tender years this was a startling spectacle and one hardly knew where to look. Where not to look was plain to all. Subsequent visits found him, hope on hope ever, still there and still at it. Not a cricket-lover, evidently.

In the charabanc *en route* for home, Mead's leg-glides gave place as a subject of conversation to our thoughts and views on the muddled divine. Could he have been, we charitably asked ourselves, quite right in the head? Unhinged in some way? Instinct told us not to discuss the matter with Matron when, that evening at bed-time, she inspected our toe-nails and indulged herself, after her lonely hours, with a few swift snippings.

Further astonishments completed a remarkable day. We were given two fried eggs each for supper, perched on a mound of sauté potatoes. This sumptuousness was without precedent and so entranced the school that the head boy automatically jumped up and gave three cheers for Mrs Macdonald, the headmaster's deaf and remote wife, whose Buff Orpingtons had strained away to produce the main item of the feast.

While we were munching the eggs and discussing, naturally, the Reverend Whosit, the door burst open and the games master entered. Respectful silence fell. His lips could be seen to be trembling. He gulped. 'I want you all to know,' he said, 'that I alone was responsible for the charabanc starting so late this morning and for your missing part of the match. I can only apologise and ask for your forgiveness.' Silence continued; even I had stopped eating. 'But, although you may find it in your hearts to forgive me, I can never forgive myself.' Pressing a handkerchief to his wobbling mouth, he hurried out.

There now! What an exciting emotional outburst to round off the day! As it happened, neither Williamson nor I had noticed that the charabanc had started late. Happily seated in the very front of the conveyance, after shrieks of 'bags I!', we had been discussing the charms of Dorothy Dickson and he had at last agreed to swop his signed photograph of her for some rather pretty and ingenious cogwheels from my Number Four Meccano set. As far as we were concerned, the charabanc need never have left at all.

To be honest, it must be confessed that the incident of the wonky clergyman was not entirely surprising to some of us. Preparatory schools at that time seemed each to have its quota of unmarried masters who were still looking about for Miss Right. Although it was difficult for them to marry on their miserable salaries, that was not, for all of them, the problem. Some of them were by nature looking about for Miss Right rather less vigorously than others. Dedicated paedophiles stalked the linoleum-covered corridors and, sensing a non-frosty reception, pounced. No boy who wasn't actually repellent could consider himself safe from an amorous mauling among the rows of pendant macintoshes. The purpose of these ungainly gymnastics was lost on the more naïve boys; they referred to the odd activities as 'romping', a verb which has since caught up with them. But I, an odious and knowing little giggling plumpness, was well aware of what was toward and realised that the merest show of cooperation would lead, sooner or later, in God's good time, somehow somewhere, to a sticky tribute. Bulls' eyes, for instance.

At school the best cricket players were loaded with honours and privileges throughout their brief years of glory, not the least of which was to see their names in print (a thrill at that age). The school magazine dutifully recorded their successes and faults.

Characters of the XI

H. R. J. VEREKER. Has 'skippered' excellently. His googlies were cleverly flighted and he has an outstanding action. His decision to promote G. J. B. Eyebright from the 'Colts' was fully justified.

G. J. B. EYEBRIGHT. An attractive bat who fully justified his promotion from the 'Colts'.

N. C. DE B. GASCOYNE. It is time he learnt not to nibble at off balls. Alert at silly mid-on but goes down rather sluggishly. Must use his head more.

Every cricket match, however dreary or disastrous, was fully reported. One dreadful term at Stirling Court when summer influenza had filled the dormitories and emptied the pavilion, we could only provide an XI to play against Dumbleton Park by pressing into service the eleven boys still on their feet. I had avoided summer influenza.

> *v.* Dumbleton Park
> Played at Stirling Court on July 3rd
> Lost by nine wickets

'. . . and was quickly "yorked" for 2. Marshall, playing a little tentatively on 0, failed to survive a confident appeal for L.B.W. and assisted in the side's rapid collapse . . .'

School magazines also featured selections of heart-lifting news of Old Boys. These were mainly garnered from the letters that we periodically wrote to the headmaster. I had, doubtless, been boasting.

> C. F. JELLINEK has joined his father's smelting works in Bradford but has managed to keep up his interest in matters philatelic. Good old Jelly!
>
> P. N. HUFFKINS is still a flautist in the Bagshot 'week-end' orchestra and has become engaged to Miss Felicity Rollmops of 'Chatsworth', Station Crescent, Reading. Our warmest wishes for a tuneful 'duet'!
>
> A. MARSHALL has been broadcasting and has got to know Phyllis Monkman.

Names such as Jellinek and Huffkins are not comfortable ones for a boy to be landed with but in the end we tired of drawing attention to their oddity. Not so with some of the Christian names that lurked safely behind such initials as H.R.J. Occasionally it became necessary, when Common Entrance and School Certificate forms were being filled in, for a boy's full names to be revealed in the open classroom, and to the consternation of their owners out tumbled the Bertrams, the Herberts, the Jaspers, the Bellamys, the Clarences, the

Augustuses, the Montmorencys, each of which was thought irresistibly droll when belonging to somebody else.

Although names were far from sacred at Stirling Court, two things were: religious observances and parents. In the dormitories, those who wished could kneel unmolested to say their prayers, and photographs of our loved ones could be proudly displayed. Even the most mocking among us were respectfully silent when gazing at the framed likenesses of Mrs Baughurst and Major Symington, smiling, pince-nezed and cabinet-size.

On one occasion, Mrs Baughurst gave a vast picnic beanfeast for the entire school, goodies galore. She kindly came down herself for the affair and dispensed tea and iced lemonade, and smiles and chuckles to go with them. Her flowered dress reminded me of a cretonne sofa cover. She was enormously fat. Everything that could bulge, bulged. In due course, when we were all pleasantly replete, the head boy called for three cheers for Mrs Baughurst, but later at supper he was heard to say that he really ought to have called for three chairs for Mrs Baughurst. Though some of us thought this a witty quip and secretly admired it, it was generally found to be in very poor taste. It met with a chilly reception and for some days the head boy was not spoken to.

Humorists were not, as a general rule, encouraged. After the matchless *Bulldog Drummond*, which we all read once a term, our favourite reading was *Tarzan of the Apes*, by Edgar Rice Burroughs. At Stirling Court we had a boy called Edgar and when one day at lunch we had rice pudding, he seized his spoon and, plunging it into his heaped plate, said merrily, 'Edgar burrows in the rice.' Not particularly funny yet harmless enough and we laughed obligingly as we usually did (hoping for correspondingly jolly cackles when we ourselves were inspired to be witty). But the joke was by no means harmless in the eyes of the master at the head of the table. We were told to stop laughing and poor Edgar had to finish his lunch standing up (much more of a torment than it sounds) and was not allowed to bathe in the sea for a week, a typically bizarre and inappropriate scholastic punishment.

Another unfortunate humorous occurrence took place at Dumbleton Park, whither we had had to walk (two miles) in a surly, shuffling crocodile to watch yet another cricket match. A large, non-playing Dumbletonian, a well-known wag called Montefiore, politely sought to divert the visitors. He was wearing a tight white sweater and up inside it he inserted two cricket balls where a woman's breasts would, in his opinion, be. Looking very improbable, he then paraded mincingly up and down before our section of the spectators. He was a huge success. Our delighted laughter rang out, and some of us even applauded. As a spectacle, the cricket didn't stand an earthly.

At the close of play we scuffed our way back to Stirling Court and were just beginning our supper when the headmaster appeared, looking very far from genial. 'Which of you laughed at Montefiore and his disgusting exhibition?' There was a long, frightened silence. 'Stand up any boy who laughed at Montefiore!' More silence, and then a single victim courageously rose from his seat. It was Williamson, *noblesse oblige*. The rest of us, cowards to a boy, strove to look as though we had been deeply shocked by Montefiore.

Williamson was beaten just before evening prayers. By the time the summons came for him to go to the headmaster's study, he had transformed himself into the tragic person of Charles I going forth to his execution. Nothing could have been more regal as he strode from the room, patting a head here, a cheek there. 'Grieve ye not, good my peoples,' he said, passing solemnly through the door, 'and when I am gone, pray you, look to the Queen.' When he returned shortly after, rather pink in the face, Charles I had been forgotten. 'Only three, and they didn't hurt a bit.' It was characteristic of his generous nature to bear us no grudge for not owning up with him.

At my public school, you got off one afternoon's cricket a week by enlisting in the OTC. There were two parades a week and though the less lovely episodes of my years as a private are still vivid in the mind, it was just worth it. For the afternoon parade we struggled into some elaborate pieces of webbing and buckle in the armoury's dark recesses and were soon dressing by the right. Being on the plump side, I was difficult to align. I was the last to stop shuffling forwards or backwards, obligingly sticking out this or pulling in that and trying, in my friendly way, to help. There was then a good deal of marching about in fours and, chatting *sotto voce* to a neighbour, it was fatally easy to mishear words of command and to be discovered executing a faultless left incline while the others were busy right wheeling. One's little blunders were pointed out, in a stream of verbal discourtesies, by NCOs and a pained look only drove them to further excesses.

Once a term the OTC staged a mass outing known as a Field Day. More often than not in driving sleet from the east, we marched down to the railway station, the School Fife and Bugle Band doing, one supposes, its best to keep our spirits up. I wore a pair of thick and disapproved-of gloves to protect the chilblains that were an occupational risk of school life in bracing Northamptonshire.

With all the *joie de vivre* of slave labour bound for Siberia, we entrained and, in a third-class carriage, found ourselves gazing at a coloured view of The Promenade, Eastbourne. I had to insist on a corner-seat for, like some rare old wine, I did not travel well and nobody had yet invented Kwells. However, it was the work of a moment to rattle down the window and do what stern Nature demanded. Whenever we chugged through some wayside halt, I could be relied upon to leave behind a splashy greeting.

These activities were unpopular but all was forgiven and forgotten when we detrained near some blasted heath and marched bravely forth, clutching our sandwiches and spoiling for battle. The opposing force, after a train journey, tended to be either Rugby or Stowe. Sometimes we didn't even catch a glimpse of them, though the distant popping of blanks led one

to believe they were somewhere about. When there was no
train but a march of five miles, the enemy was invariably
Uppingham. These, on one occasion, we did see. The leading
sections met each other head on in the middle of a turnip field.
The sight of the delicious bomb-like vegetable was too much
and soon the nutritious roots were flying to and fro, scoring
delightfully noisy direct hits. The officers seemed to miss the
fun of the thing and, after we had downed turnips and dressed
by the right ('Back a little, Marshall'), we were given a fearful
wigging. But never mind. We hadn't had to play cricket.

If I seem to harp on cricket, it is only because in one's youth
there was such a terrible amount of it. I estimate that during
my passage through the 1920s, 2,000 hours, or about eighty-
four days and nights, or twelve whole weeks of my life were
spent, longing to be elsewhere, in flanelled gloom in the
middle of a field. But no, I am wrong. Luckily enough it was
not always in the middle of the field but more towards the side
of it. Having, at Stirling Court, proved myself a butterfingers
at anything calling for speedy action and initiative near the
batsman and wicket, I spent a comparatively peaceful two
years in a position well known at preparatory schools but
without, I feel, any official recognition. I refer to the key post
of Long Stop. It is to be found immediately behind the wicket-
keeper (at Stirling Court, the wicket was kept, naturally, by
Williamson) towards the boundary of the field of play and it
has much to recommend it.

Socially it was agreeable as it allowed you to pass the time of
day with friends enjoying nougat nearby, but its chief charm
lay in the fact that there was only one chance in five of you ever
being drawn into the unlovely cricketing picture. The ball
when bowled might hit the batsman, the batsman might hit it,
it might hit the wicket, it might hit the wicket-keeper. When it
missed all these hazards and came rolling towards you, you

found yourself in the very thick of the game. Old hands like myself, however, felt no need to panic. The grass in the outfield was by nature long and lush and if it had not recently been mown, there was a good chance of the ball coming to a halt before it even reached you. No point in meeting trouble halfway. Ignoring unmannerly shouts to run, you waited for the ball to come to rest and then, hurrying briskly forward, you picked it up and threw it in, thus skilfully preventing the batsmen from crossing for the fifth time.

At school we faced the tyranny of cricket, and of all games, in the same uncomplaining way that we faced surds, fractions, Canada's exports, Euclid, Tasmania's imports, and the Hundred Years' War. It was all part of the scholastic merry-go-round, part of Life's rich pattern. Daily we put on those hot and unsuitable cricketing togs, the bags supported by a school belt with snake clasp. On our heads we placed those enormous shapeless grey felt bonnets without which small boys were thought to succumb instantly from sunstroke, and out on to the field we trooped for a generous three hours of the national game.

Beneath a tree stood the visible scoring apparatus, a selection of white numbers on sheets of black tin hung on a discarded blackboard and mysteriously known as the Tallywag. The boys who worked this were a sort of walking wounded, boys recovering from boils or headaches or lunch or asthmatic attacks and they had behind them a long tradition of indolence and lack of cooperation. They lay on their stomachs chewing wine-gums and reading another chapter of *The Black Gang*. When they tired of that, they would just aimlessly hit each other for five minutes or so. From time to time, a despairing cry of 'TALLYWAG' would reach them from the pitch, and they would then reluctantly change the tin plates to a score that was possibly accurate to the nearest ten. At the end of play, they were allowed by old custom to leave the Tallywag showing a somewhat improbable result to the game (999 for 1, last man 998).

At public schools, the summer term ended with a week at an OTC camp. To get to the camp we, of course, entrained, and after prolonged discomfort reached a tented enclosure, often at one or other of those trying Tidworths (Park or Pennings). The moment we arrived, and with not a second to freshen up or take a restorative, we were barked at by the red-tabbed regular officer in command ('Here to work . . . no shilly-shallying . . . put your backs into it . . .'), addressed by the padre ('See you at Church Parade . . . sing up . . . put your backs into it') and given by the medical officer some superfluous hygienic hints. We were then free to inspect our roomy quarters.

Not much caring for the feel of blankets upon the bare skin, I had had constructed at home a sleeping-bag of old sheets. This comforting device caused unaccountable rage (jealousy, I can only suppose) but nobody could think of any reason for withdrawing it. But, sheeted or not, sleep under canvas was not easily come by. To discourage conversation, the officers went about thwacking with their sticks on the tent sides but all that this noisy show did was to awaken the earwigs. Sensing intruders, they scurried up to the top of the tent-pole and then, with a do-or-die abandon, hurled themselves down on to one's face. After the last wave had gone in, the ants took over. And when their work was done, the rain, in a gentle patter, began.

For the more sensitive digestions, the camp food was chancy. It was prepared without the hand of love in black apparatus that had the look of being salvage from the Crimea. Not that the officers were indifferent. Indeed, they were for ever bursting in at meal-times and inquiring whether there were any complaints. One boy, not realizing that this was a purely formal question requiring nothing but glum despair by way of answer, once drew attention to some culinary mishap or other — a dead mouse in the stew or some such bagatelle. Everyone was very shocked (not, of course, about the mouse) and nobody complained again.

The washing arrangements were very far from ideal, and

about certain other arrangements I prefer not to speak. By way of drawing attention officially to their unsavoury primitiveness, they were usually burnt down on the last night of camp and provided a cheering spectacle. An opportunity was made in the morning for us to be reprimanded about this, after we were, naturally, nicely in line ('Up a little, Marshall'), but at the final breakfast nobody bothered to ask us if we had any complaints for how could we have? We were going home.

The admirable length of the summer holidays prevented one from thinking very much about the forthcoming winter term and what lay ahead in the form of Rugby football. But Rugby football did have one small silver lining — you could occasionally lie down and take a short rest. Of course, it wasn't called lying down and resting. It was known as 'falling on the ball' to stop the opposing forwards dribbling it, and it was an entirely brave and praiseworthy action. It usually caused a loose scrum to be formed over your inert body and so your resting period was sometimes quite prolonged. The ground might be damp but exertion was momentarily over. Pleasantly relaxed and outstretched, one could ponder on this and that — the universe, the eternal mysteries, or which delicacy was being prepared for house supper at 7 p.m. I did a lot of falling on the ball. 'Well fallen, Marshall' a kindly captain would cry, drawing attention to my selfless pluck. While lying down one sometimes got a football boot in the face but then everything here below has its price.

In the summer holidays there were still a lot of games. Parents tended to think that juvenile social life could not move happily forward without games. And so out of doors we played tennis and croquet and golf and badminton, and indoors there was bridge, bezique, halma, chess, happy families, mah-jongg, and a pencil-and-paper game called Consequences which provided pleasurable fantasies such as 'Stanley Baldwin met Gladys Cooper in the Taj Mahal'.

I rather enjoyed the tennis parties. For these the sun seemed

always to shine. They began at 3 p.m. and everybody was
dressed entirely in white, though ladies were permitted a
coloured Suzanne Lenglen bandeau to keep their shingles in
position, and the belts that supported the gentlemen's flannels
could, at a pinch, be dark blue. On the very tick of three, you
alighted from your bicycle, shook hands with your hostess
('*How* you've shot up, Arthur! School seems to suit you!') and
then, with the other guests, you stood gazing at the tennis
court which old Hawker had freshly marked out with
wavering hand and tottering feet.

In those days, the tennis posts were not such reliable
contrivances as they are now and on really damp courts
(vicarage ones were, for some reason, especially sodden) the
softness of the earth and the tension of the net caused the posts
to lean amorously towards each other. Geometrically, this
lowers the height of the net. Here there was no question of a
white band in the middle to keep the net down. The whole
problem was how to keep it up and it was quite in order to prop
the centre of the net with a sort of metal prong. If there were no
prong, an agonized and embarrassed daughter of the house
might sometimes whisper to her mother that she thought the
net was sagging. The reply was firm and simple: 'Erica, it is
not sagging. Now, hurry up all of you, you're wasting precious
sunlight.'

If you were fortunate, you would find upon the tennis court
six tennis balls, never one more, and frequently one less. They
had been in service since the beginning of the season and were
now dark green in colour and, though light in weight from
constant use, were strangely reluctant to bounce very high.
Sometimes they had been smeared with tennis-shoe whitening
so that the first few shots covered you with exciting explosions
of white dust. Then they went dark green again. On a table in
a shady spot (under the cedar, if cedar there were) stood the
refreshment, a large jug of home-made lemonade, than which
there is nothing nicer, covered with a piece of butter-muslin to
discourage flies and hemmed with beads to keep it in place.

There were deck chairs scattered about and a rug or two (a large bundle of rugs sometimes turned out to contain an elderly relation, wheezing encouragement), and some of those old-fashioned racquet presses that look like mediaeval contraptions for helping reluctant persons to speak up.

The number of players for one court was usually ten, so you had to get as fond of sitting down and talking as of playing. When the main body of guests had arrived ('I think poor old Gregory must have got a puncture'), and the hostess had made mention of what a lovely day they had brought with them, she would then say 'Now, how will you play? Who'll start?' This was the cue for everybody to put on a condemned look and shout simultaneously 'Oh no, I'd much rather sit out. Please, Mrs Bancroft, truly.' In the end, four players were chivied on to the court, where they all set up a wailing moan of 'Well, I must be given the best player because I'm absolutely putrid, no really I am.'

The tennis playing itself was a sort of ritual. It bristled with ceremony and complications and observances and rules of behaviour. For example, if you did a particularly good service, what one might gaily call an 'ace', the accepted thing was to assume that your opponent wasn't looking and hadn't prepared himself. 'I say, were you ready?' you called, to which the invariable answer was 'Yes, but not for that!' Merry chuckles. If a ball came down the centre of the court, or anywhere near it, you and your partner both screeched 'Yours, partner' and then leapt away from the ball as though it were a hand grenade just fizzing to a conclusion. To rush towards such a ball would have been to lay yourself open to the serious charge of 'poaching'. Poaching wasn't popular; poachers' names became known and then poachers weren't asked again.

Shots that looked as though they had fallen just out of court had to be sportingly announced as having fallen just in ('No, honestly Helen, I'm quite quite sure'). Not a moment passed without some sort of comment from somebody and the air rang with 'Good shot', 'Hard luck', 'Well tried' and 'Oh I say, *I* didn't think it was coming over either'. If there was a spirited rally, with the ball changing sides as often as five or six times, somebody was sure to give a jolly cry of 'Why go to Wimbledon?' Shots of unintentional brilliance, such as a dazzling backhand sliced smash off the racquet handle and part of one's thumb, had to be apologised for for minutes on end. When a ball was carelessly struck and flew out of court and into the flowers, that was the signal for all the spectators to rise, to say in unison 'All right, I'll get it', and then to move off in a sort of mass migration and start trampling down the lupins.

Play halted during this manœuvre while all the players gathered at the nearest point behind the stop-netting and yelled conflicting instructions: 'Further in, Cyril', '*Much* more to your right', 'Now, Muriel, walk straight towards me'. If a ball was lost during the last hour of play, the hostess would say 'Never mind, we'll look for it later', which explains why there were sometimes five balls instead of six.

The first set after tea (home-made cakes, huge slices of wafer-thin bread-and-butter, ginger snaps, Earl Grey) was always a men's four, the ladies being thought to be too distended with macaroons to be able to move with any ease or pleasure. So they sat out and dabbed their mouths with the handkerchiefs that had been tucked into the gold bangles which they wore just above the left elbow.

Later on, the master of the house would sometimes return from work and could occasionally be coaxed by his wife into taking part: 'I think that if we spoke *really* nicely to Herbert he might be persuaded to join you in a final set.' Loyal cries of 'Hooray!' from the guests, and ten minutes or so later the genial and beflanelled host would reappear from the house shouting something comical such as 'Lead on, Macduff', or 'Will one of you young chaps lend me a bat?' And then, after his efforts had turned him a deep and rather worrying purple colour, and despite everybody's co-operation he had lost the set 6–0, there would start up the usual preparations for goodbye — 'Just look at the time', 'I must really fly: we've got Aunt Honor coming to dinner'. And in a flurry of thank-yous, it was on to one's bicycle and away. And if one hadn't poached, there would probably be another tennis party the very next day.

Even the most high-spirited boys experienced a feeling of wretchedness and doom when returning to Stirling Court for the winter term. We were as dejected as Mrs Macdonald's Michaelmas daisies which by now were covered in cobwebs and sea-mist and general dankness and were the only one of Nature's vegetable wonders currently visible from the class-room windows. Williamson himself, seldom one to flag, looked listless, even in the year when he had returned from the summer holidays with a splendid new fantasy. He imagined that the entire royal family had been annihilated by some giant *machine infernale* which had exploded at a royal wedding. After diligent search, the authorities discovered that the nearest surviving relative (2,845th in succession) was a Mrs Denise Harrison, living in somewhat questionable circumstances in Maida Vale (in a hotel where men stayed for only quite short periods of time) and no stranger to strong waters. She comes to the throne and is speedily known as Queen Denise the Damned. Constantly drunk, she appears at odd hours on the balcony, blowing kisses and making unsuitable gestures. At the Coronation service, she drinks off the Communion wine in one gulp, demands cocktails as a chaser, waves tipsily from the coach and, reaching out a hand, drags into it a Scots guardsman and draws the curtains. After a short while, his trousers are ejected. She dies, hopelessly dotty and intoxi-cated, while trying to fondle the Archbishop of Canterbury. This pleasurable improbability did cheer us all for a few days.

When the first endless fortnight had come to a close, it was only the beginning of October, with two full months and most of December still to go. Life was a drab procession of dreadful Latin and French irregular verbs (among them, poor old *ouïr*, of which so little seemed to exist). The French sentences we translated were always either full of unreality ('This rake is mine but whose hoes are those?') or non-sequiturs ('My hands are very sore but I am richer than you think').

Still, there were always the new boys to persecute and bombard with cricketing riddles:

Who was the first cricketer in the Bible?
Don't know.
St Peter.
Why?
He stood up before the eleven and was bold.
Oh.

Who bowled fewest balls in the Bible?
Don't know.
The eunuchs.
Why?
They hadn't any.
Oh.

Why is a tie like a telescope?
Don't know.
Because it pulls out.

On this occasion the 'Oh' was more of a shriek for when the miserable boy's tie was pulled out, it was frequently attached to his shirt by a tie-clip so that the front part of the shirt came out too. And, deeply humiliated and unaccustomed to this kind of jollity, he dared not blub until he had got safely into a lavatory.

To savour more fully the pleasure of not having to play cricket, we would often run over the high points of the summer season. One year the sports' master had been removed, not for any of the usual reasons but with appendicitis. His replacement seemed not to care for cricket and to do nothing but sit in the shade and read and this withdrawal gave a boy called Mould a chance to shine. He was very small and rather weasel-like and he had become an expert bowler of high-speed sneaks, varying them with those balls of alarmingly high trajectory that come dropping out of the sky like a bomb. Neither of these deliveries is recommended by the cognoscenti, but then neither of them is actually illegal and as the gentleman in the shade seemed neither to notice nor mind, Mould opened our bowling for a full six weeks. Success was immediate. To stop the sneaks (it was impossible to score from them), the very bottom of the bat had to be used. This frequently sent a painful, stinging tremor up the bat and the batsman's arms, in which case Mould would bowl the next ball instantly, usually capturing a valuable wicket. On dazzlingly sunny days, Mould's bombs took fine toll of the blinded batsmen, either in wickets or in injuries. In this manner, we had been able to trounce our dreaded rivals, Dumbleton Park, both 'at home' and 'away', while Westcliff went down like nine-pins (a total of seven, and three boys in tears).

And in addition to Mould, there was always Williamson, who went in first wicket down and whose regal deportment with the bat constantly demoralized opposing bowlers. His haughty mien put one in mind of Henry VIII and it was his habit, while the bowler was thundering down for his first ball, to cry out 'just one moment, please', and then effect a small adjustment to his clothing. But alas, when the sports' master returned, minus appendix, all was discovered, we were reprimanded for unsporting behaviour, and poor Mould was demoted to the Second XI.

One November day, another surprise treat was announced. Owing, we were told, to the kindness of the ever-generous Mrs Baughurst, we were to be shown a film in the village hall, where there was a proper projector. As the hall was in full use most afternoons (and for adult film performances in the evenings), the little excitement had to be arranged for the morning, which meant an hour or two less work. A treat indeed. The music mistress, Mrs Wakefield, had kindly consented to seat herself at the upright while the silent film was unreeling and give us of her best.

On thinking over the disaster afterwards, we came to the conclusion that Mrs Baughurst had trustingly put herself in the hands of the hall manager and had requested a film suitable for young persons, and the manager, to save money and trouble, had merely decided to show the film destined for that evening, which he probably hadn't yet seen. So, after a Pathé Gazette and a short travel film (Hungary, jerking up and down in downpours of rain), the main feature began, to a tuneful selection by Mrs Wakefield from *Merrie England*.

The film was called *Frailty, Thy Name Is . . .* and it was set in the depths of the English countryside. There were three chief characters — Farmer Giles (generously bewhiskered), Mrs Giles (considerably younger than her rustic mate), and Bob, the farm hand (considerably younger than his employer). Bob lived with the Giles's and took all his meals with them and one did just wonder why, instead of getting on with the plentiful home fare, he was spending quite so much time leering at Mrs Giles from behind a cottage-loaf.

AND THUS FOR SOME WEEKS THE BUSY FARM LIFE
CONTINUED

said the caption, and there they all were, milking cows, churning butter, feeding chickens and collecting eggs. Just a peaceful bit of old England.

AND SO TO THE NIGHT WHEN DESTINY WAS TO
WRECK THREE LIVES

it ran, and the night began with a frightful storm, with trees being blown down and every farmhouse window banging. In the morning, it was found that a section of the farmhouse thatch had come adrift and, mounting a ladder to repair it, Farmer Giles missed his footing, crashed heavily to the ground, writhed for several minutes, was examined by the doctor and carried to bed where he lay motionless and with a displeased expression, Mrs Giles being very solicitous and patting pillows.

I BE NO USE TO THEE, LASS. I CAN MOVE NEITHER
HAND NOR FOOT

Nor anything else, one was given to understand, for Bob now increased his appalling leers, and Mrs Giles, who at first had not noticed them, now started noticing them like anything.

Seated at the piano, Mrs Wakefield was out of sight of the screen and had throughout been unaware of the nature of the drama that was unfolding itself. She specialized in what was then a popular piece of pianoforte virtuosity — the *valse brillante*. This was an ordinary *valse* but with the addition of great runs and tremendous trills and bangings and much crossing of the hands. She had rightly reserved a few of the best of these for the last reels of the film and by now she was in fullest flood and producing a delightful cascade of thrilling and cheerful melody.

But what was this? Mrs Giles, as slim as a rake to start with, was visibly increasing in size, especially round the lower middle section, with Bob leering like a maniac and Farmer Giles looking grumpy and narrowing his eyes at his wife whenever she took him up his lunch. And then, unknown either to Bob or Mrs Giles (they were clearing out the hay-loft, or so they said), Farmer Giles hobbled painfully from bed and fetched his shot-gun, concealing it in a bedroom cupboard.

For some time now, there had been anxious mutterings in the hall's rear seats, where the staff were drinking in the entertainment. Now one heard people walking about and suddenly the film flickered away into darkness and the hall lights were switched on. Mrs Wakefield brought her current *valse brillante* to a reluctant close and we were all told to walk back to Stirling Court. There, after lunch, the Headmaster said that, by some mistake, we had been shown a film that was really only meant for 'grown-ups' and which we wouldn't have enjoyed (we had seen most of it) and would we please not mention the matter in our Sunday letters home, other than the bare fact that there had been a film. Doubtless something soothing and false was written to Mrs Baughurst but we were accustomed to such prudery and concealments. Williamson never let us forget that when, in his first term and during some dormitory horseplay (Drake on the bowling-green), he had broken a *pot de chambre*, the item had appeared on his end-of-term bill as 'Large teacup: five shillings'.

And thus for some weeks the busy winter term continued. Every month we had our hair cut by a hairdresser from Southsea and his lady assistant, whose unlovely task it was to shampoo our heads. For this, we repaired to the bathroom and, with towels round our necks to sop up the trickles, we bent our heads over the side of a bath. This, naturally, gave Williamson a chance for yet another Charles I decapitation performance, much to the lady's irritation ('Oh you *silly* boy!'), but he pardoned her with a regal gesture and then, to show that he had other strings to his bow, he would give his famous impression of José Collins singing 'Love will find a way' — a deafening treble rendering that the entire school, except for the staff, found entrancing.

One evening, in just such a winter term, something took place that, unknown to me at the time, was to give an unusual purpose to my life. The headmaster announced that there was to be a school debate. What a debate was had to be explained to most of us. The motion before us was something to do with public transport. The debate began. Masters spoke. Boys droned on about this and that. Probably mishearing some debating point, or idiotically misunderstanding it, I got up and said something or other, and everybody laughed, and laughed really quite loudly. I blushed, thinking I had been stupid, but I was very far from being displeased. Golly, what an *agreeable* sound, I thought, and I had, however unwittingly, caused it. I had suddenly become consciously aware of laughter and since that day I have always tried to go where laughter was, to seek laughter out, to impede laughter as little as possible, to have as friends people who could make me laugh (they have been extremely kind), to read books that provoke, either intentionally or otherwise, laughter, to see plays intended to provide laughter. I am aware that as a major aim in life this has been frivolous and petty and, maybe, rather contemptible and that I should have been worrying about the state of the world, the human condition, and poverty and famine and misery. But I am afraid that I haven't been and, I must confess, it's been great fun.